✈ AEROFILMS GUIDE

FOOTBALL
GROUNDS

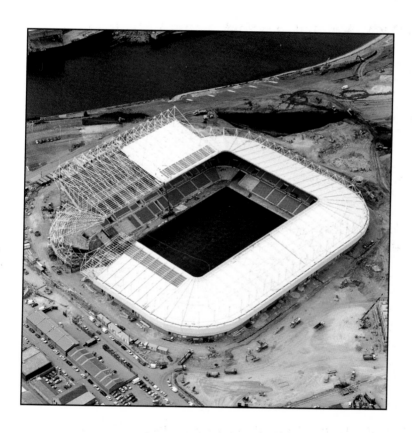

AEROFILMS GUIDE

FIFTH
REVISED
EDITION

FOOTBALL
GROUNDS

DIAL
HOUSE

CONTENTS

Preceding pages: The extremes of the new face of football for the 1997/98 season: Sunderland's new home at Monkwearmouth and Moss Rose, the home of Macclesfield Town, the newest recruit to the Nationwide Football League.

First published in 1993
Reprinted 1993 (Twice)
Second edition 1994
Third edition 1995
Fourth edition 1996
Fifth edition 1997

ISBN 0 7110 2541 X

Published by Dial House

an imprint of Ian Allan Ltd, Terminal House, Station Approach, Shepperton, Surrey TW17 8AS

Printed by Ian Allan Printing Ltd, Coombelands House, Addlestone, Weybridge, Surrey KT15 1HY

Aerial photography ©

Aerofilms

Hunting Aerofilms Limited have been specialists in aerial photography since 1919. Their library of aerial photographs, both new and old, is in excess of 1.5 million images. Aerofilms undertake to commission oblique and vertical survey aerial photography which is processed and printed in their specialised photographic laboratory. Digital photomaps are prepared using precision scanners. The Company has been a subsidiary of Hunting plc since 1936.

Free photostatic proofs are available on request for any site held within the collection and price lists will be forwarded detailing the sizes of photographic enlargement available without obigation to purchase.

Text © Ian Allan Ltd 1993, 1994, 1995, 1996, 1997
Football action photography © Empics
Photographs of Wembley reproduced by kind permission of Wembley plc

Editor's Note

Welcome to the fifth edition of *Aerofilms Guide: Football Grounds*. As in previous editions we have tried to ensure that the book has recorded all the changes to have affected FA Carling Premiership and Nationwide League grounds over the past year. As always, however, the speed of modern construction means that some work, particularly on the new grounds, will be further advanced than the specially taken aerial photographs illustrate.

This fifth edition records no less than six new grounds; five of these — Bolton Wanderers, Derby County, Oxford United, Stoke City and Sunderland — are brand-new stadia replacing older grounds. The sixth — Macclesfield Town — is the result of the Champions from the Vauxhall Conference being promoted. As a result of Macclesfield's triumph we have to bid farewell to Hereford United; few football fans will forget the drama of the last weekend of the 3rd Division season when Brighton, needing either a draw or a win to retain league status after a highly troubled season, scraped home 1-1 at Edgar Street, thereby consigning Hereford to the Conference.

Mention of Brighton & Hove Albion draws attention to a potential problem. Having sold the Goldstone Ground, Brighton are now homeless although the new consortium behind the club is hopeful that a new stadium will be built to replace it. Following a period of uncertainty, it was announced in June that the club was going to play its home games at Gillingham for a two-year period with an option for a third if necessary; this was, however, changed only a few days later by an announcement that Millwall was now the preferred option. We have chosen to illustrate Millwall's ground as the Brighton entry and hope that this is not further overtaken by events. The new consortium has, however, been told by the Football League that the club must return to the Brighton area within three years. The club has plans for a new £25 million stadium at Waterhall on the outskirts of the town.

Each year we think that the process of ground modernisation will come to an end; each year we are proved wrong. The next 12 months will see work take place at, inter alia, Darlington and Liverpool, whilst the trend towards new purpose-built stadia also continues, with Reading being the next to move. Following the vote of supporters, Everton too will make a move away from its traditional home whilst there are also strong indications that, if Arsenal can't get permission to develop Highbury, the club will move away.

No doubt all these new stands and stadia are superb, but there is a danger that football will start to lose its traditions. The corollary of all the new work is that old stadia and terraces — with all their history and folklore — will disappear. It will be a great loss if some of these are not preserved for future generations.

We hope that you will have an enjoyable football season.

Disabled Facilities

We endeavour to list the facilities for disabled spectators at each ground. Readers will appreciate that these facilities can vary in number and quality and that, for most clubs, pre-booking is essential. Some clubs also have dedicated parking for disabled spectators; this again should be pre-booked if available.

WEMBLEY

Wembley Stadium, Wembley HA9 0DW

Tel No: 0181-902 8833
Advance Tickets Tel No: 0181-900 1234
Fax: 0181-900 1055
Brief History: Inaugurated for F.A. Cup Final of 1923, venue for many major national and international matches including World Cup Final of 1966. Also used for major occasions in other sports and as venues for rock concerts and other entertainments.
(Total) Current Capacity: 79,000 (all seated)
Nearest Railway Station: Wembley Complex (BR), Wembley Central (BR & Tube), Wembley Park (tube)

Parking (Car): Limited parking at ground and nearby
Parking (Coach/Bus): As advised by police
Police Force: Metropolitan
Anticipated Development(s): It has been confirmed that Wembley has been selected for redevelopment as the national stadium for football and rugby league. The work will entail the rebuilding of virtually the entire existing stadium with only the twin towers surviving from the original stadium.

ARSENAL

Arsenal Stadium, Avenell Road, Highbury, London, N5 1BU

Tel No: 0171 704 4000
Advance Tickets Tel No: 0171 704 4040
Fax: 0171 704 4001
League: F.A. Premier
Brief History: Founded 1886 as Royal Arsenal, changed to Woolwich Arsenal in 1891, and Arsenal in 1914. Former grounds: Plumstead Common, Sportsman Ground, Manor Ground (twice), moved to Arsenal Stadium (Highbury) in 1913. Record attendance 73,295
(Total) Current Capacity: 38,900 (all seated)
Visiting Supporters' Allocation: 1,800 (all seated)
Club Colours: Red shirts with white sleeves, white shorts
Nearest Railway Station: Drayton Park & Finsbury Park. Arsenal (tube)

Parking (Car): Street Parking
Parking (Coach/Bus): Drayton Park
Police Force and Tel No: Metropolitan (0171 263 9090)
Disabled Visitors' Facilities
  Wheelchairs: Lower tier East Stand
  Blind: Commentary available
Anticipated Development(s): With its capaci limited to 39,000, Arsenal's ground is significantly smaller than many of the other leading Premiership teams. It has been repor that, unless the club gets permission to redevelop part of the existing stadium — whic is difficult given its confined location amongs residential property — it will seek to relocate a new greenfield site.

KEY

C Club Offices
E Entrance(s) for visiting supporters

⬆ North direction (approx)

❶ Avenell Road
❷ Highbury Hill
❸ Gillespie Road
❹ To Drayton Park BR Station (¼ mile)
❺ Arsenal Tube Station
❻ Clock End

Left:
A somewhat strange season for the Gunners saw Bruce Rioch unceremoniously dumped as Manager before the season started and the Frenchman Arsene Wenger eventually appointed to replace him. Although Arsenal's challenge in the various cup competitions was short-lived, the club continued to threaten for the Premiership title until the very end of the season. One factor in the team's league success was the goalscoring of England international Ian Wright.

ASTON VILLA

Villa Park, Trinity Road, Birmingham, B6 6HE

Tel No: 0121 327 2299
Advance Tickets Tel No: 0121 327 5353
Fax: 0121 322 2107
League: F.A. Premier
Brief History: Founded in 1874. Founder Members Football League (1888). Former Grounds: Aston Park and Lower Aston Grounds & Perry Barr, moved to Villa Park (a development of the Lower Aston Grounds) in 1897. Record attendance 76,588
(Total) Current capacity: 39,300 (all seated)
Visiting Supporters' Allocation: Approx. 3,086 in North Stand Lower Tier (R Block) and North Stand RR Block
Club Colours: Claret with blue stripe shirts, white shorts.

Nearest Railway Station: Witton
Parking (Car): Asda car park, Aston Hall Roa
Parking (Coach/Bus): Asda car park, Aston Hall Road (special coach park for visiting supporters situated in Witton Lane).
Police Force and Tel No: West Midlands (01 322 6010)
Disabled Visitors' Facilities
 Wheelchairs: Trinity Road Stand section
 Blind: Commentary by arrangement
Anticipated Development(s): The Trinity Road Stand is being reroofed and other plans envisage the ground's capacity eventually bein increased to 50,000.

KEY

C Club Offices
S Club Shop
E Entrance(s) for visiting supporters
R Refreshment bars for visiting supporters
T Toilets for visiting supporters

↑ North direction (approx)

❶ B4137 Witton Lane
❷ B4140 Witton Road
❸ Trinity Road
❹ A4040 Aston Lane to A34 Walsall Road
❺ To Aston Expressway & M6
❻ Holte End
❼ Visitors' Car Park

Left:
Whilst never really challenging for major honours, Villa reached the upper echelons of the Premiership and guaranteed themselves a place in the 1997/98 UEFA Cup. The season was not, however, without its controversial moments for the club; Mark Bosnich's Nazi-style salute and disputes between the club and certain high-profile players being but part of a colourful year for the team. Captain Andy Townsend makes a typically aggressive run in this Premiership match against Leeds United on 19 October 1996.

BARNET

Underhill Stadium, Westcombe Drive, Barnet, Herts, EN5 2BI

Tel No: 0181 441 6932
Advance Tickets Tel No: 0181 441 6932
Fax: 0181 447 0655
League: 3rd Division
Brief History: Founded 1888 as Barnet Alston. Changed name to Barnet (1919). Former grounds: Queens Road & Totteridge Lane. Promoted to Football League 1991. Record attendance 11,026.
(Total) Current capacity: Approx. 4,000 (approx 1,800 seated)
Visiting Supporters' Allocation: 915 in South Stand (uncovered) with 450 overflow in East Terrace
Club Colours: Amber & Black shirts, black shorts.

Nearest Railway Station: New Barnet (High Barnet - Tube)
Parking (Car): Street Parking & High Barnet Station
Parking (Coach/Bus): As directed by Police
Police Force and Tel No: Metropolitan (018 200 2212)
Disabled Visitors' Facilities
  Wheelchairs: Barnet Lane (Social Club end few spaces)
  Blind: No special facility
Anticipated Development(s): There is nothing definite planned at this stage although there are rumours of a relocation. The temporary seating the South Stand installed originally for the 1995/96 season will remain again during 1997/9

KEY

C Club Offices
S Club Shop
E Entrance(s) for visiting supporters
R Refreshment bars for visiting supporters
T Toilets for visiting supporters

↑ North direction (approx)

❶ Barnet Lane
❷ Westcombe Drive
❸ A1000 Barnet Hill
❹ New Barnet BR Station (1 mile)
❺ To High Barnet Tube Station, M1 & M25

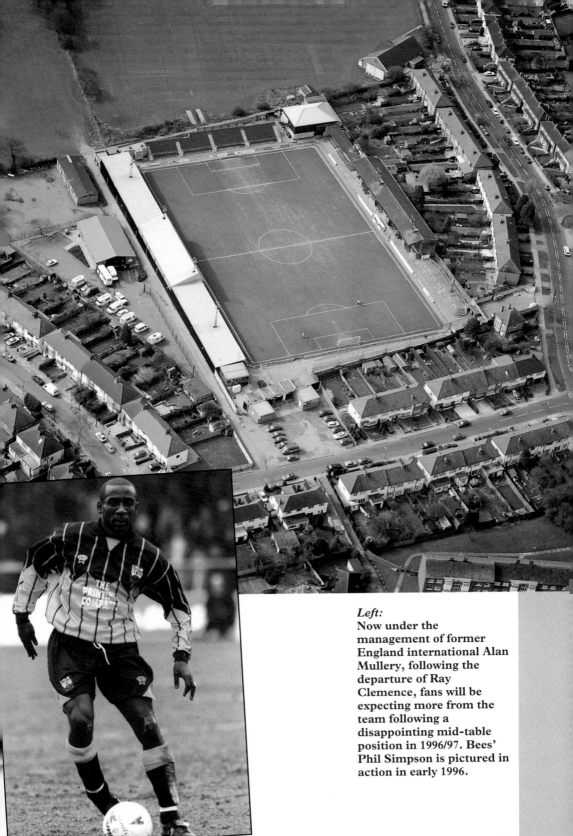

Left:
Now under the management of former England international Alan Mullery, following the departure of Ray Clemence, fans will be expecting more from the team following a disappointing mid-table position in 1996/97. Bees' Phil Simpson is pictured in action in early 1996.

BARNSLEY

Oakwell Ground, Grove Street, Barnsley, S71 1ET

Tel No: 01226 211211
Advance Tickets Tel No: 01226 211211
Fax: 01226 211444
League: F.A. Premier
Brief History: Founded 1887 as Barnsley St Peter's, changed name to Barnsley in 1897. Former Ground: Doncaster Road, Worsboro Bridge until 1888. Record attendance 40,255.
(Total) Current capacity: 19,000 (all seated)
Visiting Supporters' Allocation: 4,322 (seating in North Stand, plus uncovered seating behind goal)
Club Colours: Red shirts, white shorts

Nearest Railway Station: Barnsley Exchange
Parking (Car): Queen's Ground car park
Parking (Coach/Bus): Queen's Ground car park
Police Force and Tel No: South Yorkshire (01226 206161)
Disabled Visitors' Facilities
  Wheelchairs: Purpose Built Disabled Stand
  Blind: Commentary available
Anticipated Development(s): With the completion of the West Stand, attention is now focused on the Spion Kop, although there are no definite plans as yet.

KEY

C Club Offices
S Club Shop
E Entrance(s) for visiting supporters
R Refreshment bars for visiting supporters
T Toilets for visiting supporters

↑ North direction (approx)

❶ A628 Pontefract Road
❷ To Barnsley Exchange BR station and M1 Junction 37 (two miles)
❸ Queen's Ground Car Park

Right:

After 110 years Barnsley finally achieved the ultimate in achieving promotion to the top flight at the end of the 1996/97 season. Whilst most pundits will probably see the team as certainties for relegation back to the 1st Division, Danny Wilson and his team will no doubt take encouragement from the success of Wimbledon and the three teams promoted at the end of the 1995/96 season. The Tykes' Nicky Eaden is pictured in 1st Division action against Southend on 7 December '96.

BIRMINGHAM CITY

St Andrew's, St. Andrew's Street, Birmingham, B9 4NH

Tel No: 0121 772 0101
Advance Tickets Tel No: 0121 772 0101
Fax: 0121 766 7866
League: 1st Division
Brief History: Founded 1875, as Small Heath Alliance. Changed to Small Heath in 1888, Birmingham in 1905, Birmingham City in 1945. Former Grounds: Arthur Street, Ladypool Road, Muntz Street, moved to St Andrew's in 1906. Record attendance 68,844.
(Total) Current Capacity: 25,000 (all seated)
Visiting Supporters' Allocation: 3,600
Club Colours: Blue shirts, White shorts

Nearest Railway Station: Birmingham New Street
Parking (Car): Street parking
Parking (Coach/Bus): Coventry Road
Police Force and Tel No: West Midlands (01 772 1169)
Disabled Visitors' Facilities
Wheelchairs: 20 places; advanced notice required.
Blind: No special facilities.
Anticipated Development(s): Nothing defini but the next stage in any redevelopment will involve the Railway End.

KEY

C Club Offices
S Club Shop
E Entrance(s) for visiting supporters
R Refreshment bars for visiting supporters
T Toilets for visiting supporters

↑ North direction (approx)

❶ Car Park
❷ B4128 Cattell Road
❸ Tilton Road
❹ Garrison Lane
❺ To A4540 & A38 (M)
❻ To City Centre and New Street BR Station (1¹/2 miles)

16

ight:

season of promise for City — gh-profile Manager (Trevor rancis) and a host of new signings uch as Steve Bruce) — suggested at the team would be amongst the vourites for one of the automatic romotion places. In the event, ity spent most of the season in the rong half of the table and never ally fulfilled their potential. No oubt David Sullivan and Karren rady will be expecting a great deal ore from their expensive squad in 97/98. Paul Furlong is seen aying in the 1st Division local erby against Wolverhampton anderers on 17 November 1996.

BLACKBURN ROVERS

Ewood Park, Blackburn, Lancashire, BB2 4JF

Tel No: 01254 698888
Advance Tickets Tel No: 01254 671666
Fax: 01254 671042
E-Mail: enquiries@rovers.co.uk
League: F.A. Premier
Brief History: Founded 1875. Former Grounds: Oozebooth, Pleasington Cricket Ground, Alexandra Meadows. Moved to Ewood Park in 1890. Founder members of Football League (1888). Record attendance 61,783.
(Total) Current Capacity: 31,367 (all seated)
Visiting Supporters' Allocation: 3,800 at the Darwen End

Club Colours: Blue & white halved shirts, whi shorts
Nearest Railway Station: Blackburn
Parking (Car): Street parking
Parking (Coach/Bus): As directed by Police
Police Force and Tel No: Lancashire (01254 51212)
Disabled Visitors' Facilities
  Wheelchairs: All sides of the ground
  Blind: Commentary available.
Anticipated Development(s): None anticipat

KEY

C Club Offices
S Club Shop
E Entrance(s) for visiting supporters
R Refreshment bars for visiting supporters
T Toilets for visiting supporters

⬆ North direction (approx)

❶ A666 Bolton Road
❷ Kidder Street
❸ Nuttall Street
❹ Town Centre & Blackburn Central BR Station (1½ miles)
❺ To Darwen and Bolton
❻ Car parking area for 500 cars
❼ Car Parks
❽ Top O'Croft Road

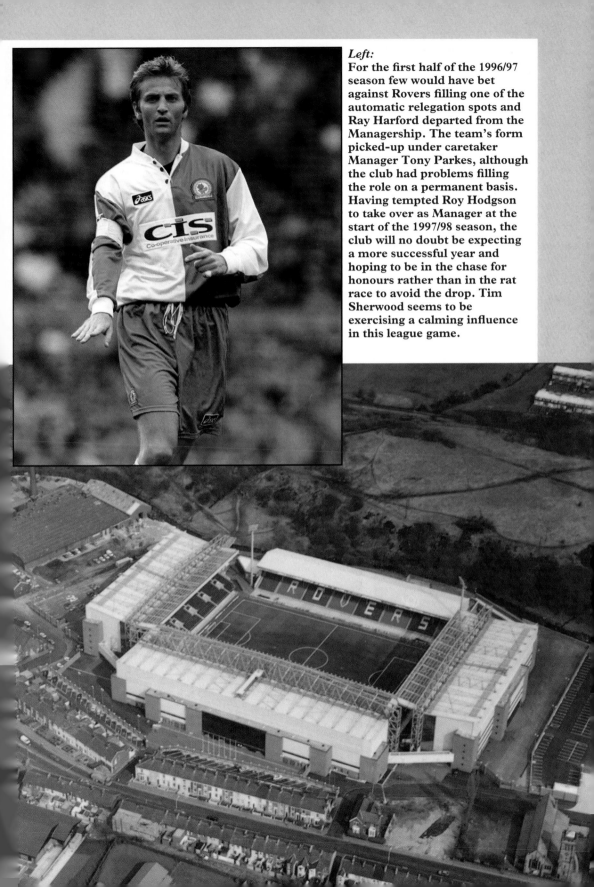

Left:

For the first half of the 1996/97 season few would have bet against Rovers filling one of the automatic relegation spots and Ray Harford departed from the Managership. The team's form picked-up under caretaker Manager Tony Parkes, although the club had problems filling the role on a permanent basis. Having tempted Roy Hodgson to take over as Manager at the start of the 1997/98 season, the club will no doubt be expecting a more successful year and hoping to be in the chase for honours rather than in the rat race to avoid the drop. Tim Sherwood seems to be exercising a calming influence in this league game.

BLACKPOOL

Bloomfield Road, Blackpool, Lancashire, FY1 6JJ

Tel No: 01253 405331
Advance Tickets Tel No: 01253 404331
Fax: 01253 405011
E-Mail: bfc@cyberspace.net
League: 2nd Division
Brief History: Founded 1887, merged with 'South Shore' (1899). Former grounds: Raikes Hall (twice) and Athletic Grounds, Stanley Park. South Shore played at Cow Cap Lane, moved to Bloomfield Road in 1899. Record attendance 38,098
(Total) Current Capacity: 11,047 (3,036 seated)
Visiting Supporters' Allocation: 2,300 approx. (none seated)
Club Colours: Tangerine shirts, tangerine shorts
Nearest Railway Station: Blackpool South

Parking (Car): At Ground & street parking (also behind West Stand - from M55)
Parking (Coach/Bus): Mecca car park (behind North End,
(also behind West Stand - from M55)
Police Force and Tel No: Lancashire (01253 293933)
Disabled Visitors' Facilities
  Wheelchairs: By players entrance
  Blind: No special facility
Anticipated Development(s): The plans for a relocation seem to have gone on 'hold'. It is likely that the club will remain at Bloomfield Road for at least two years and there is a possibility that this ground will receive attention if the plans for a new stadium fall through.

KEY
C Club Offices
E Entrance(s) for visiting supporters
S Club Shop
R Refreshment bars for visiting supporters
T Toilets for visiting supporters

⬆ North direction (approx)

❶ Car Parks
❷ To Blackpool South BR Station (1/2 mile) and M55 Junction 4
❸ Bloomfield Drive
❹ Central Drive
❺ Henry Street
❻ Blackpool Greyhound Stadium
❼ Blackpool Tower

Left:
Pipped at the post by Bristol City for one of the 2nd Division Play-Off spots, Blackpool will face a further season in the lower division. Andy Preece is pictured in a pre-season friendly against Darlington on 10 August 1996.

BOLTON WANDERERS

Reebok Stadium, Mansell Way, Horwich, Bolton, BL6 6JW

Tel No: (Reebok Stadium) 01204 698800
Tel No: 01204 389200*
Advance Tickets Tel No: 01204 521101*
Fax: 01204 366882*
* Note that these are the numbers of Burnden Park and no decision has as yet been made about transferring them to the new ground.
E-Mail: admin@bolton.u-net.com
League: FA Carling Premiership
Brief History: Founded 1874 as Christ Church; name changed 1877. Former grounds: Several Fields, Pikes Lane (1880-1895) and Burnden Park (1895-1997). Moved to Reebok Stadium for 1997/98 season. Founder-members of the Football League (1888). Record attendance (Burnden Park): 69,912
(Total) Current Capacity: 25,000 (all-seater)
Visiting Supporters' Allocation: 5,200 (South Stand)

Club Colours: White shirts, blue shorts
Nearest Railway Station: Lostock Junction
Parking (Cars): 2,000 places at ground with u to 3,000 others in proximity
Parking (Coach/Bus): As directed
Police Force and Tel No: Greater Mancheste (01204 522466)
Disabled Visitors' Facilities
  Wheelchairs: c200 places around the groun
  Blind: Commentary available
Anticipated Development(s): With the new ground nearing completion, the club has no further plans at this stage. Note that if the ne ground is not completed by the start of the season the team will possibly play its first hor match at Maine Road.

KEY

↑ North direction (approx)

❶ Junction 6 of M61
❷ A6027 Horwich link road
❸ South Stand (away)
❹ North Stand
❺ Nat Lofthouse Stand
❻ West Stand
❼ M61 northbound to M6 and Preston
❽ M61 southbound to Manchester
❾ To Horwich and Bolton
❿ To Lostock Junction BR station

Left:
Following their relegation from the Premiership at the end of the 1995/96 season, Wanderers started their campaign in the 1st Division determined to bounce back immediately. Dominating the division, the club won the championship by some 20 clear points, ensuring that the first season in the new stadium would be in the top flight. One factor in the club's success was the scoring record of John McGinlay, seen in action here on 2 March 1997 in the 1st Division match against West Bromwich Albion.

A.F.C. BOURNEMOUTH

Dean Court, Bournemouth, Dorset BH7 7AF

Tel No: 01202 395381
Advance Tickets Tel No: 01202 395381
Fax: 01202 309797
League: 2nd Division
Brief History: Founded 1890 as Boscombe St. John's, changed to Boscombe (1899), Bournemouth & Boscombe Athletic (1923) and A.F.C. Bournemouth (1971). Former grounds: Kings Park (twice) and Castlemain Road, Pokesdown. Moved to Dean Court in 1910. Record attendance 28,799.
(Total) Current Capacity: 10,500 (3,140 seated)
Visiting Supporters' Allocation: 2,770 (150 seated Family Stand only).
Club Colours: Red/Black and white pinstripe shirts, white shorts.

Nearest Railway Station: Bournemouth
Parking (Car): Large car park adjacent groun
Parking (Coach/Bus): Large car park adjacen ground
Police Force and Tel No: Dorset (01202 552099)
Disabled Visitors' Facilities
Wheelchairs: South Stand (prior arrangement)
Blind: No special facility
Anticipated Development(s): The club hope — should it survive (which is by no means certain at the time of writing) — that it will b occupying a new stadium by the start of the 1998/99 season.

KEY

C Club Offices
S Club Shop
E Entrance(s) for visiting supporters
R Refreshment bars for visiting supporters
T Toilets for visiting supporters

↑ North direction (approx)

❶ Car Park
❷ A338 Wessex Way
❸ To Bournemouth BR Station (1½ miles)
❹ To A31 & M27
❺ Thistlebarrow Road
❻ King's Park Drive
❼ Littledown Avenue
❽ A3049 Ashley Road

Right:

In a season dominated by financial problems, the fact the club survived at all is perhaps more important than the lowly position it achieved in the 2nd Division. However, with the future now more secure as Britain's first community football club, fans will be hoping to see the club aim higher. Marcus Oldbury seems perplexed by events during this 2nd Division game in early 1996.

BRADFORD CITY

The Pulse Stadium, Valley Parade, Bradford, BD8 7DY

Tel No: 01274 773355
Advance Tickets Tel No: 01274 770022
Fax: 01274 773356
E-Mail: brafordcityfc@compuserve.com
League: 1st Division
Brief History: Founded 1903 (formerly Manningham Northern Union Rugby Club founded in 1876). Continued use of Valley Parade, joined 2nd Division on re-formation. Record attendance 39,146.
(Total) Current Capacity: 18,018 (10,748 seated)
Visiting Supporters' Allocation: 1,840 (all seated)
Club Colours: Claret & amber shirts, black shorts
Nearest Railway Station: Bradford Forster Square

Parking (Car): Street parking and car parks
Parking (Coach/Bus): As directed by Police
Police Force and Tel No: West Yorkshire (01274 723422)
Disabled Visitors' Facilities
    Wheelchairs: Sunwin (ex-N&P) Stand
    Blind: No special facility
Anticipated Development(s): With the completion of the Midland Road stand, Valle Parade is now a four-sided stadium. The clu now planning to replace the standing area on the Kop — one of the largest standing areas in the English game — with a two-level stand accommodate a similar number of supporter order to fulfil the requirements of the Taylor Report.

KEY

C Club Offices
E Entrance(s) for visiting supporters
S Club Shop

⬆ North direction (approx)

❶ Midland Road
❷ Valley Parade
❸ A650 Manningham Lane
❹ To City Centre, Forster Square and Interchange BR Stations M606 & M62
❺ To Keighley
❻ Car Parks
❼ Sunwin Stand
❽ Midland Stand

ght:

he 1st Division was always going to be
struggle for the Bantams following
eir Wembley triumph at the end of
e 1995/96 season. Despite cup glory at
verton, where the mercurial Chris
addle showed why he had become a
m favourite with the City faithful,
ost of the season was a constant battle
ainst relegation, a battle which was
ccessfully won with a 3-0 home win
er QPR in the last game of the
ason. Veteran striker Carl Shutt
mpetes for the ball in the away game
Port Vale on 29 September 1996,
hen City both scored its first away
al and also achieved its first away
int.

BRENTFORD

Griffin Park, Braemar Road, Brentford, Middlesex, TW8 0NT

Tel No: 0181 847 2511
Advance Tickets Tel No: 0181 847 2511
Fax: 0181 568 9940
E-Mail: brentford@digibase.demon.co.uk
League: 2nd Division
Brief History: Founded 1889. Former Grounds: Clifden House Ground, Benn's Field (Little Ealing), Shotters Field, Cross Roads, Boston Park Cricket Ground, moved to Griffin Park in 1904. Founder-members Third Division (1920). Record attendance 39,626.
(Total) Current Capacity: 12,922 (9,079 seated)
Visiting Supporters' Allocation: 2,263 (636 seated)

Club Colours: Red & White striped shirts, bla[ck] shorts
Nearest Railway Station: Brentford Central, South Ealing (tube)
Parking (Car): Street parking (restricted)
Parking (Coach/Bus): Layton Road car park
Police Force and Tel No: Metropolitan (018[1] 577 1212)
Disabled Visitors' Facilities
   Wheelchairs: Braemar Road
   Blind: Commentary available
Anticipated developments(s): The club plan[s] to redevelop the Ealing Road Terrace but the[re] are also long term plans to build a brand new stadium away from Griffin Park.

KEY

C Club Offices
S Club Shop
E Entrance(s) for visiting supporters
R Refreshment bars for visiting supporters
T Toilets for visiting supporters

⬆ North direction (approx)

❶ Ealing Road
❷ Braemar Road
❸ Brook Road South
❹ To M4 (1/4 mile) & South Ealing Tube Station (1 mile)
❺ Brentford Central BR Station
❻ To A315 High Street & Kew Bridge

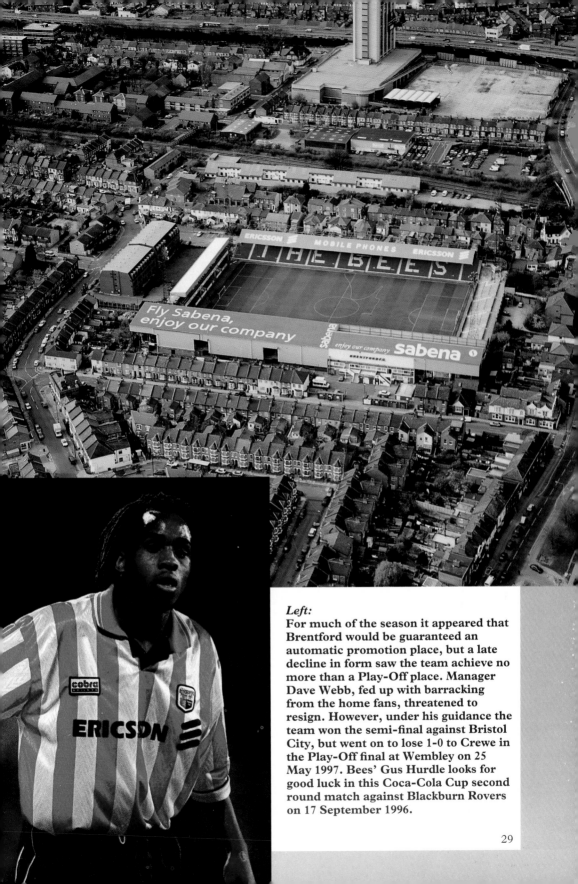

Left:

For much of the season it appeared that Brentford would be guaranteed an automatic promotion place, but a late decline in form saw the team achieve no more than a Play-Off place. Manager Dave Webb, fed up with barracking from the home fans, threatened to resign. However, under his guidance the team won the semi-final against Bristol City, but went on to lose 1-0 to Crewe in the Play-Off final at Wembley on 25 May 1997. Bees' Gus Hurdle looks for good luck in this Coca-Cola Cup second round match against Blackburn Rovers on 17 September 1996.

29

BRIGHTON & HOVE ALBION

New Den, Bolina Road, London, SE16 3LN

Tel No: (Millwall) 0171 232 1222
Advance Tickets Tel No: 01273 778855
League: 3rd Division
Brief History: Founded 1900 as Brighton & Hove Rangers, changed to Brighton & Hove Albion 1902. Former grounds: Home Farm (Withdean), County Ground, Goldstone Ground (1902-1997). Ground-share with Millwall pending construction of a new stadium in Brighton. Founder members of the 3rd Division (1920). Record attendance (Goldstone Ground): 36,747.
(Total) Current Capacity: 20,150
Visiting Supporters' Allocation: To be confirmed.
Club Colours: Blue and white striped shirts and blue shorts
Nearest Railway Station: South Bermondsey

BR station or Surrey Quays tube — East London Line (service temporarily suspended)
Parking (Cars): Juno Way car park (8min walk)
Parking (Coach/Bus): At ground
Police Force and Tel No: Metropolitan (0171 679 9217)
Disabled Visitors' Facilities
  Wheelchairs: West Stand lower tier
  Blind: Commentary available
Anticipated Development(s): Following the sale of the Goldstone Ground, Brighton was homeless and a number of options were considered. The club signed a deal to share facilities at the New Den (having earlier negotiated an arrangement to groundshare with Gillingham). The club hopes to complete a new £25 million stadium at Waterhall (on Brighton's outskirts) within two years.

KEY

C Millwall club offices
S Millwall club shop
E Entrance(s) for visiting supporters

Club Address:
18 Queen's Road,
Brighton, BN1 3XG
Tel: 01273 778855
Fax: 01273 321095
Shop Address:
6 Queen's Road,
Brighton

⬆ North direction (approx)

❶ Bolina Road
❷ South Bermondsey BR station
❸ To Surrey Quays Underground station
❹ Zampa Road
❺ Ilderton Road
❻ To Rotherhithe New Road and Rotherhithe Tunnel
❼ To New Cross
❽ Surrey Canal Road

Left:

A disastrous season for the Seagulls saw them rooted to the bottom of the 3rd Division for virtually all the year until they finally overhauled Hereford at the end of a tense game at Edgar Street in the final match of the season; needing a draw or a win to survive, Brighton achieved a 1-1 draw, thereby consigning Hereford to the Vauxhall Conference. Penalised two points by the FA for crowd trouble and facing the certain loss of the Goldstone Ground, Brighton's season was marked more by internecine strife than success on the field. Pictured during the all-important match at Hereford on 3 May 1997 is Brighton's Robbie Reinelt. The team's survival owed much to the appointment of Steve Gritt as Manager; at the time he took the job few would have expected the team to retain its league position.

BRISTOL CITY

Ashton Gate, Winterstoke Road, Ashton Road, Bristol, BS3 2JI

Tel No: 0117 963 0630
Advance Tickets Tel No: 0117 966 6666
Fax: 0117 963 0700
League: 2nd Division
Brief History: Founded 1894 as Bristol South End changed to Bristol City in 1897. Former Ground: St John's Lane, Bedminster, moved to Ashton Gate in 1904. Record attendance 43,335
(Total) Current Capacity: 21,000 (all seated)
Visiting supporters' Allocation: 2,500 (all seated)

Club Colours: Red shirts, white shorts
Nearest Railway Station: Bristol Temple Meads
Parking (Car): Street parking
Parking (Coach/Bus): Marsh Road
Police Force and Tel No: Avon/Somerset (0117 927 7777)
Disabled Visitors' Facilities
  Wheelchairs: Advanced notice not required
  Blind: Commentary available
Anticipated Development(s): None anticipated.

KEY
C Club Offices
S Club Shop
E Entrance(s) for visiting supporters

↑ North direction (approx)

❶ A370 Ashton Road
❷ A3209 Winterstoke Road
❸ To Temple Meads Station (1½ miles)
❹ To City Centre, A4, M32 & M4

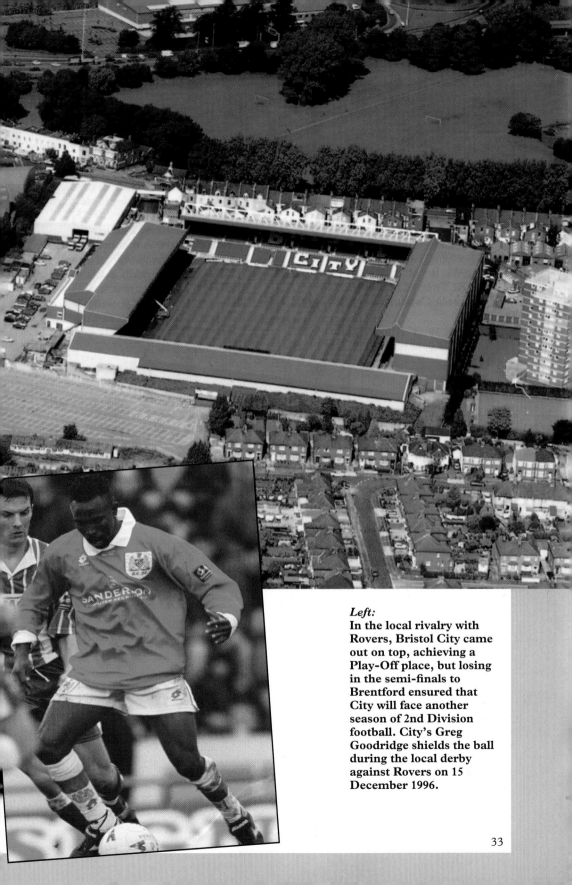

Left:
In the local rivalry with
Rovers, Bristol City came
out on top, achieving a
Play-Off place, but losing
in the semi-finals to
Brentford ensured that
City will face another
season of 2nd Division
football. City's Greg
Goodridge shields the ball
during the local derby
against Rovers on 15
December 1996.

33

BRISTOL ROVERS

The Memorial Ground, Filton Avenue, Horfield, Bristol BS7 0A

(Registered Office: The Beeches, Broomhill Road, Brislington, Bristol BS4 5BF)

Tel No: 0117 977 2000

Advance Tickets Tel No: 0117 977 2000

Fax: 0117 977 3888

League: 2nd Division

Brief History: Founded 1883 as Black Arabs, changed to Eastville Rovers (1884), Bristol Eastville Rovers (1896) and Bristol Rovers (1897). Former grounds: Purdown, Three Acres, The Downs (Horfield), Ridgeway, Bristol Stadium (Eastville), Twerton Park (1986-1996), The Memorial Ground 1996. Record attendance: (Eastville) 38,472, (Twerton Park) 9,813, (Memorial Ground) 8,078.

(Total) Current Capacity: 8,975 (1,871 seated); standing capacity of 7,104 includes 500 on the Family Terrace due to open during 1997/98.

Visiting Supporters' Allocation: 740 (Centena Stand Terrace)

Club Colours: Blue & white quartered shirts, wh shorts

Nearest Railway Station: Filton or Stapleton R

Parking (Cars): Limited parking at ground for home fans only; street parking also available

Parking (Coach/Bus): As directed

Police Force and Tel No: Avon/Somerset (0117 927 7777)

Disabled Visitors' Facilities:
  Wheelchairs: 35 wheelchair positions
  Blind: Limited provision

Anticipated Development(s): With the construction of the West Stand there is talk tha roof may be provided over the clubhouse terrac The Football Club is also still contemplating th construction of its own stadium in Bristol.

KEY

C Rugby Club offices

E Entrance(s) for visiting supporters

R Refreshment bars for visiting supporters

T Toilets for visiting supporters

↑ North direction (approx)

❶ Filton Avenue
❷ Gloucester Road
❸ Muller Road
❹ To Bristol city centre (2.5 miles) and BR Temple Meads station (3 miles)
❺ Downer Road
❻ Ashley Down Road
❼ To M32 J2 (1.5 miles)
❽ Strathmore Road
❾ To Filton (1.5 miles)
❿ Centenary Stand
⓫ Car Park
⓬ West Stand

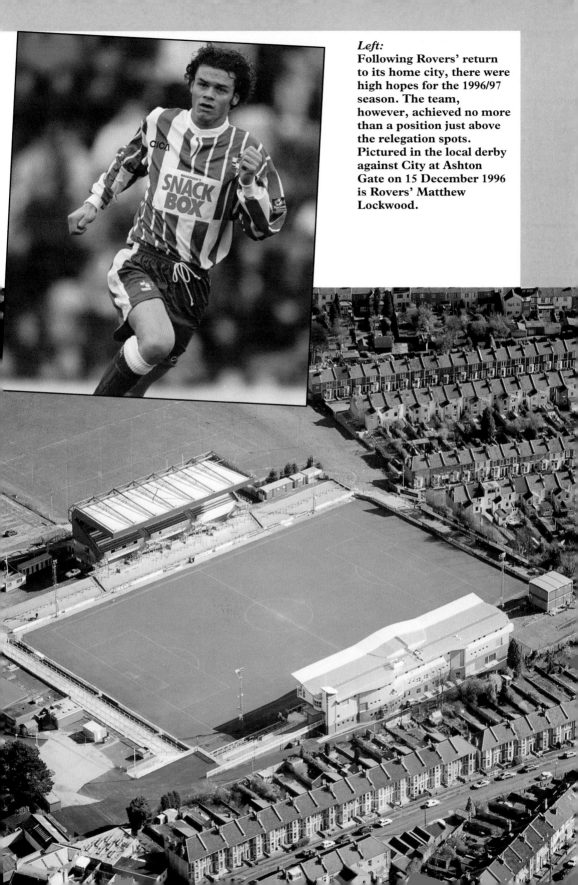

Left:
Following Rovers' return to its home city, there were high hopes for the 1996/97 season. The team, however, achieved no more than a position just above the relegation spots. Pictured in the local derby against City at Ashton Gate on 15 December 1996 is Rovers' Matthew Lockwood.

BURNLEY

Turf Moor, Brunshaw Road, Burnley, Lancs, BB10 4BX

Tel No: 01282 700000
Advance Tickets Tel No: 01282 700010
Fax: 01282 700014
League: 2nd Division
Brief History: Founded 1882, Burnley Rovers (Rugby Club) combined with another Rugby Club, changed to soccer and name to Burnley. Moved from Calder Vale to Turf Moor in 1882. Founder-members Football League (1888). Record attendance 54,775.
(Total) Current Capacity: 22,500 (all seated)
Visiting Supporters' Allocation: 4,125 (all seated in Endsleigh Stand)
Club Colours: Claret with blue sleeved shirts, white shorts

Nearest Railway Station: Burnley Central
Parking (Car): Church Street and Fulledge R (car parks)
Parking (Coach/Bus): As directed by Police
Police Force and Tel No: Lancashire (01282 425001)
Disabled Visitors' Facilities
  Wheelchairs: Bob Lord Stand – Pre-match applications
  Blind: Headsets provided with commentary.
Anticipated Development(s): Following completing of the new stand on the site of the old Bee Hole Terrace, the next stage in any redevelopment will cover the Endsleigh Stand but nothing is confirmed at this stage.

KEY
C Club Offices
E Entrance(s) for visiting supporters
S Club Shop

⬆ North direction (approx)

❶ Brunshaw Road
❷ Belvedere Road
❸ Burnley Central BR Station (1/2 mile)
❹ Cricket Ground
❺ Endsleigh Stand
❻ East Stand
❼ Bob Lord Stand
❽ North Stand

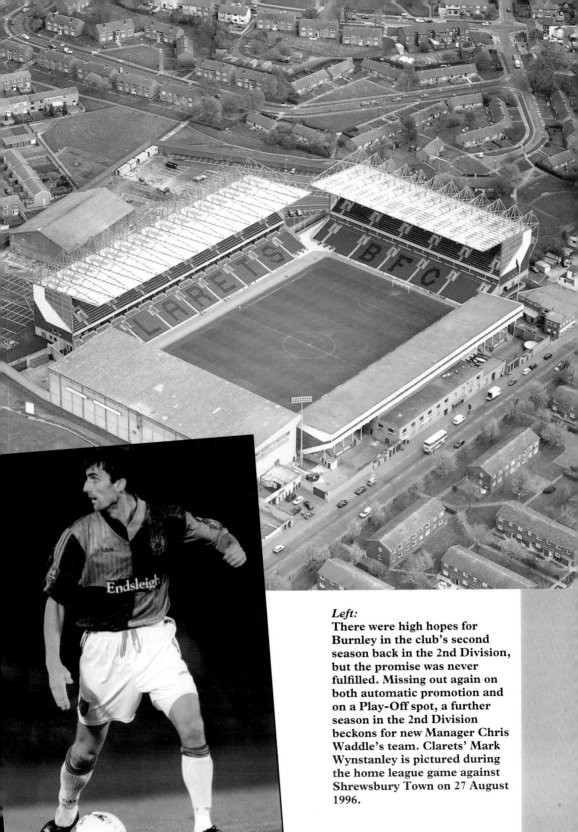

Left:

There were high hopes for Burnley in the club's second season back in the 2nd Division, but the promise was never fulfilled. Missing out again on both automatic promotion and on a Play-Off spot, a further season in the 2nd Division beckons for new Manager Chris Waddle's team. Clarets' Mark Wynstanley is pictured during the home league game against Shrewsbury Town on 27 August 1996.

BURY

Gigg Lane, Bury, Lancashire, BL9 9HR

Tel No: 0161 764 4881
Advance Tickets Tel No: 0161 764 4881
Fax: 0161 764 5521
League: 1st Division
Brief History: Founded 1885, no former names or former grounds. Record attendance 35,000
(Total) Current Capacity: 11,869 (9,369 seated)
Visiting Supporters' Allocation: 2,675 (all seated) in West Stand
Club Colours: White shirts, royal blue shorts
Nearest Railway Station: Bury Interchange

Parking (Car): Street parking
Parking (Coach/Bus): As directed by Police
Police Force and Tel No: Greater Manchester (0161 872 5050)
Disabled Visitors' Facilities
Wheelchairs: South Stand(home) and West Stand (away)
Blind: Commentary available
Anticipated Development(s): The new completion date for the redevelopment of the Cemetery End is 1998.

KEY

- **C** Club Offices
- **S** Club Shop
- **E** Entrance(s) for visiting supporters
- **R** Refreshment bars for visiting supporters
- **T** Toilets for visiting supporters

↑ North direction (approx)

- **❶** Car Park
- **❷** Gigg Lane
- **❸** A56 Manchester Road
- **❹** Town Centre & Bury Interchange (Metrolink) (³⁄₄ mile)

Left:
A triumphant season for the Shakers saw Bury achieve its second successive promotion, this time as the champions of the 2nd Division. Astutely managed by Stan Ternent, the team took the title ahead of fellow northwest team Stockport County. Bury's Dean West runs with the ball during the final Nationwide League game of the season against Millwall — one of the pre-season favourites for promotion — after which the triumphant team was presented with the 2nd Division trophy.

CAMBRIDGE UNITED

Abbey Stadium, Newmarket Road, Cambridge, CB5 8LN

Tel No: 01223 566500
Advance Tickets Tel No: 01223 566500
Fax: 01223 566502
League: 3rd Division
Brief History: Founded 1913 as Abbey United, changed to Cambridge United in 1949. Former Grounds: Midsummer Common, Stourbridge Common, Station Farm Barnwell (The Celery Trenches) & Parker's Piece, moved to Abbey Stadium in 1933. Record attendance 14,000.
(Total) Current Capacity: 9,617 (3,242 seated)
Visiting Supporters' Allocation: 2,316 (366 seated)
Club Colours: Amber and black shirts, black shorts
Nearest Railway Station: Cambridge (2 miles)

Parking (Car): Coldhams Common
Parking (Coach/Bus): Coldhams Common
Police Force and Tel No: Cambridge (01223 358966)
Disabled Visitors' Facilities
  Wheelchairs: Limited number that should b[e] pre-booked
  Blind: No special facility
Anticipated Development(s): Although nothing is as yet confirmed, it looks more like[ly] that the club will relocate rather than redevel[op] the existing ground.

KEY
- **C** Club Offices
- **S** Club Shop
- **E** Entrance(s) for visiting supporters
- **R** Refreshment bars for visiting supporters
- **T** Toilets for visiting supporters

↑ North direction (approx)

❶ A1134 Newmarket Road
❷ To A11 & Newmarket
❸ To City Centre, Cambridge BR Station (2 miles) & M11
❹ Whitehill Road

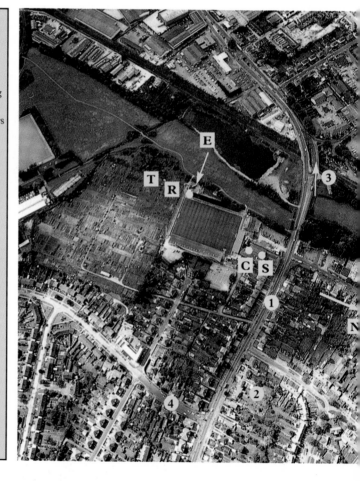

Left:
**Just missing out on the
Play-Off positions,
Cambridge United will
again face 3rd Division
opposition in 1997/98.
United's Matthew Joseph is
seen in action during the
3rd Division match against
Leyton Orient on 4 May
1996.**

CARDIFF CITY

Ninian Park, Sloper Road, Cardiff, CF1 8SX

Tel No: 01222 398636
Advance Tickets Tel No: 01222 398636
Fax: 01222 341148
E-Mail: ccscl@aol.com
League: 3rd Division
Brief History: Founded 1899. Former Grounds: Riverside Cricket Club, Roath, Sophia Gardens, Cardiff Arms Park & The Harlequins Rugby Ground, moved to Ninian Park in 1910. Ground record attendance 61,566 (Wales v. England, 1961)
(Total) Current Capacity: 13,920 (11,681 seated)
Visiting Supporters' Allocation: 939 (Grandstand Blocks A+B); can be increased by 2,239 (Grangetown End) if required

Club Colours: Blue shirts, white shorts
Nearest Railway Station: Ninian Park (adjacent) (Cardiff Central 1 mile)
Parking (Car): Opposite Ground, no street parking around ground
Parking (Coach/Bus): Sloper Road
Police Force and Tel No: South Wales (0122 222111)
Disabled Visitors' Facilities
  Wheelchairs: Corner Canton Stand/Popular Bank (covered)
  Blind: No special facility
Anticipated Development(s): Nothing defini planned.

KEY

C Club Offices
E Entrance(s) for visiting supporters
R Refreshment bars for visiting supporters
T Toilets for visiting supporters (Terrace only, when used)
S Club Shop

↑ North direction (approx)

❶ Sloper Road
❷ B4267 Leckwith Road
❸ Car Park
❹ To A4232 & M4 Junction 33 (8 miles)
❺ Ninian Park Road
❻ To City Centre & Cardiff Central BR Station (1 mile)
❼ To A48 Western Avenue, A48M, and M4 Junctions 32 and 29
❽ Ninian Park BR station

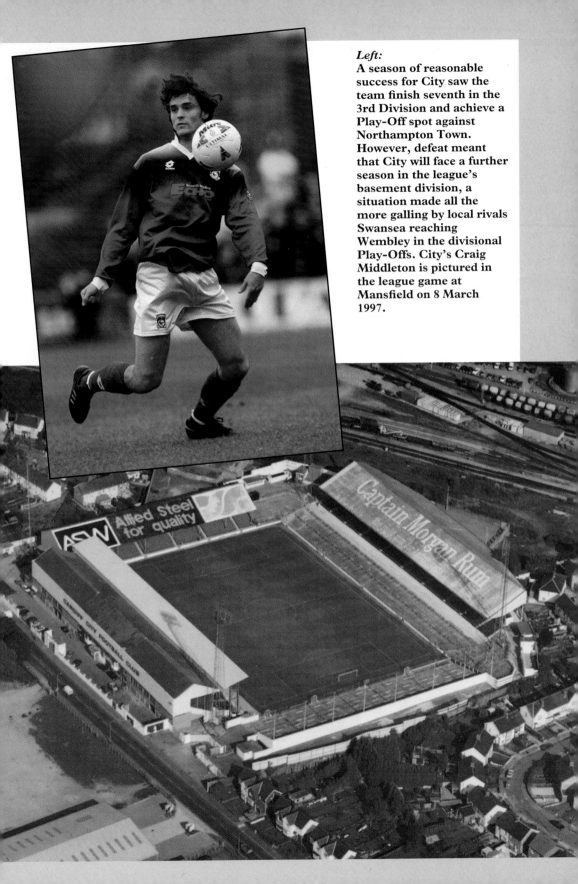

Left:
A season of reasonable success for City saw the team finish seventh in the 3rd Division and achieve a Play-Off spot against Northampton Town. However, defeat meant that City will face a further season in the league's basement division, a situation made all the more galling by local rivals Swansea reaching Wembley in the divisional Play-Offs. City's Craig Middleton is pictured in the league game at Mansfield on 8 March 1997.

CARLISLE UNITED

Brunton Park, Warwick Road, Carlisle, CA1 1LL

Tel No: 01228 26237
Advance Tickets Tel No: 01228 24014
Fax: 01228 30138
League: 2nd Division
Brief History: Founded 1904 as Carlisle United (previously named Shaddongate United). Former Grounds: Millholme Bank and Devonshire Park, moved to Brunton Park in 1909. Record attendance 27,500.
(Total) Current capacity: 16,650 (7,986 seated)
Visiting Supporters' Allocation: 2,000 (East Stand blocks 1 to 4)
Club Colours: Royal blue shirts, white shorts

Nearest Railway Station: Carlisle Citadel
Parking (Car): Rear of ground
Parking (Coach/Bus): St Aiden's Road car park
Police Force and Tel No: Cumbria (01228 28191)
Disabled Visitors' Facilities
  Wheelchairs: Front of Main Stand (prior arrangement)
  Blind: No special facilities
Anticipated Development(s): Long term plan for a 28,000 all-seater stadium, but nothing concrete planned after completion of the new East Stand.

KEY

C Club Offices
E Entrance(s) for visiting supporters
R Refreshment bars for visiting supporters
T Toilets for visiting supporters

↑ North direction (approx)

❶ A69 Warwick Road
❷ To M6 Junction 43
❸ Carlisle Citadel BR Station (1 mile)
❹ Greystone Road
❺ Car Park

Left:
Following the disappointment of relegation at the end of the 1995/96 season, Carlisle United bounced right back and achieved automatic promotion from the 3rd Division. This time the team's triumph was capped by victory in the final of the Auto Windscreen Cup Final at Wembley against Colchester. Is Michael Knighton's grand plan to get Carlisle back to the top flight back on course? Only time will tell. Here Carlisle's Rod Thomas battles with Colchester's David Gregory during their Wembley encounter on 20 April 1997.

CHARLTON ATHLETIC

The Valley, Floyd Road, Charlton, London, SE7 8BL

Tel No: 0181 333 4000
Advance Tickets Tel No: 0181 333 4010
Fax: 0181 333 4001
E-Mail: info@charlton-athletic.co.uk
League: 1st Division
Brief History: Founded 1905. Former grounds: Siemens Meadows, Woolwich Common, Pound Park, Angerstein Athletic Ground, The Mount Catford, Selhurst Park (Crystal Palace FC), Boleyn Ground (West Ham United FC), The Valley (1919-1923, 1924-85, 1992-). Founder Members 3rd Division South. Record attendance 75,031.
(Total) Current Capacity: 16,000 all seated
Visiting Supporters' Allocation: 3,073 (all seated)

Club Colours: Red shirts, white shorts
Nearest Railway Station: Charlton
Parking (Car): Street parking
Parking (Coach/Bus): As directed by Police
Police Force and Tel No: Metropolitan (018 853 8212)
Disabled Visitors' Facilities
  Wheelchairs: East/West Stands
  Blind: Commentary, 12 spaces.
Anticipated Development(s): The club has announced that it will start the construction of a new West Stand during the summer of 199 This will accommodate 8,000 in two tiers and take the capacity of the Valley to over 20,000 Scheduled opening date is some point during the 1997/98 season.

KEY
C Club Offices
E Entrance(s) for visiting supporters

↑ North direction (approx)

❶ Harvey Gardens
❷ A206 Woolwich Road
❸ Valley Grove
❹ Floyd Road
❺ Charlton BR Station
❻ River Thames
❼ Thames Barrier

Left:
Following Charlton's success in reaching the Play-Offs at the end 1995/96 season, fans were no doubt expecting the team to go one stage further and reclaim the club's position in the Premiership. Unfortunately, the promise of the previous season went unfulfilled and the team spent much of the season in the 1st Division's lower half. Addicks' Bradley Allen is pictured in the away game at Molyneux against Wolves on 6 September 1996.

CHELSEA

Stamford Bridge, Fulham Road, London, SW6 1HS

Tel No: 0171 385 5545
Advance Tickets Tel No: 0171 386 7799
Fax: 0171 381 4831
League: F.A. Premier
Brief History: Founded 1905. Admitted to
Football League (2nd Division) on formation.
Stamford Bridge venue for F.A. Cup Finals
1919-1922. Record attendance 82,905.
(Total) Current capacity: 33,000 (all seated)
Visiting Supporters' Allocation: Approx. 1,600
(East Stand Lower; can be increased to 3,200 if
required)
Club Colours: Blue shirts, blue shorts
Nearest Railway Station: Fulham Broadway
Parking (Car): Street parking

Parking (Coach/Bus): As directed by Police
Police Force and Tel No: Metropolitan (017
385 1212)
Disabled Visitors' Facilities
  Wheelchairs: East Stand
  Blind: No special facility
Anticipated Development(s): The start of th
1997/98 season will see the opening of the ne
5,000-seat Shed Stand and also the 6,000-se
lower tier of the West Stand. This latter figur
will later rise to 8,000. Work on the upper tie
of the West Stand — which has yet to be
finalised — will increase capacity by a further
7,000.

KEY	
C	Club Offices
S	Club Shop
E	Entrance(s) for visiting supporters

↑ North direction (approx)

❶ A308 Fulham Road
❷ Central London
❸ Fulham Broadway Tube
   Station
❹ Mathew Harding Stand
❺ East Stand
❻ West Stand (being
   redeveloped)
❼ South (Shed) Stand

Left:

In Ruud Gullit's first season as Manager of Chelsea, it seemed as though the entire Italian national team was playing for the club. One of a trio of Italian stars was Gianfranco Zola, whose goalscoring skills were to assist the team to reach the FA Cup final — where the team triumphed over Middlesbrough — and also to England's home defeat in the World Cup qualifier at Wembley. Here he is seen celebrating his first goal against Sunderland on 16 March 1997.

CHESTER CITY

The Deva Stadium, Bumpers Lane, Chester, CH1 4LT

Tel No: 01244 371376
Advance Tickets Tel No: 01244 371376
Fax: 01244 390265
League: 3rd Division
Brief History: Founded 1884 from amalgamation of Chester Wanderers and Chester Rovers. Former Grounds: Faulkner Street, Lightfoot Street, Whipcord Lane, Sealand Road, Moss Rose (Macclesfield Town F.C.), moved to Deva Stadium in 1992. Record attendance (Sealand Road) 20,500.
(Total) Current Capacity: 6,000 (3,408 seated)

Visiting Supporters' Allocation: 1,896 max (seated 600 max.)
Club Colours: Blue/White striped shirts, White shorts
Nearest Railway Station: Chester (3 miles)
Parking (Car): Car park at ground
Parking (Coach/Bus): Car park at ground
Police Force and Tel No: Cheshire (01244 350222)
Disabled Visitors' Facilities
    Wheelchairs: West and East Stand
    Blind: Facility available

KEY

C Club Offices
S Club Shop
E Entrance(s) for visiting supporters
R Refreshment bars for visiting supporters
T Toilets for visiting supporters

↑ North direction (approx)

❶ Bumpers Lane
❷ To City Centre and Chester BR Station (1½ miles)
❸ Car Park

50

Left:
A season of promise for City saw the team reach the Play-Off semi-finals, where they were beaten over the two legs by Swansea City. Supporters will no doubt be expecting the team to reclaim its 2nd Division spot in 1997/98. Kevin Noteman shields the ball during this 3rd Division encounter during early 1996.

CHESTERFIELD

Recreation Ground, Saltergate, Chesterfield, S40 4SX

Tel No: 01246 209765
Advance Tickets Tel No: 01246 209765
Fax: 01246 556799
League: 2nd Division
Brief History: Founded 1866. Former Ground: Spital Vale. Formerly named Chesterfield Town. Record attendance 30,968
(Total) Current Capacity: 8,954 (2,674 Seated)
Visiting Supporters' Allocation: 3,185 (885 seated)
Club Colours: Blue shirts, white shorts
Nearest Railway Station: Chesterfield

Parking (Car): Saltergate car park, street parking
Parking (Coach/Bus): As directed by Police
Police Force and Tel No: Derbyshire (01246 220100)
Disabled Visitors' Facilities
 Wheelchairs: Saltergate Stand
 Blind: No special facility
Anticipated Development(s): There are plans for the club to relocate to a new 12,000 capacity stadium at Wheeldon Park, but there is no confirmed date at this stage.

KEY
C Club Offices
S Club Shop
E Entrance(s) for visiting supporters
R Refreshment bars for visiting supporters
T Toilets for visiting supporters

↑ North direction (approx)

❶ Saltergate
❷ Cross Street
❸ St Margaret's Drive
❹ A632 West Bars
❺ To A617 & M1 Junction 29

COLCHESTER UNITED

Layer Road Ground, Colchester, CO2 7JJ

Tel No: 01206 508800
Advance Tickets Tel No: 01206 508802
Fax: 01206 508803
League: 3rd Division
Brief History: Founded 1937, joined Football League 1950, relegated 1990, promoted 1992. Record attendance 19,072.
(Total) Current Capacity: 7.920 (1,877 Seated)
Visiting Supporters' Allocation: 1,342
Club Colours: Royal Blue and white shirts, White shorts

Nearest Railway Station: Colchester Town
Parking (Car): Street parking
Parking (Coach/Bus): Boadicea Way
Police Force and Tel No: Essex (01206 7622
Disabled Visitor' Facilities
  Wheelchairs: Space for six in front of terrace (next to Main Stand)
  Blind: Space for 3 blind persons and 3 guide
Anticipated Development(s): Nothing definitely planned at this stage following completion of the Clock Street Stand.

KEY

C Club Offices
S Club Shop
E Entrance(s) for visiting supporters
R Refreshment bars for visiting supporters
T Toilets for visiting supporters

⬆ North direction (approx)

❶ B1026 Layer Road
❷ Town Centre & Colchester Town BR Station (2 miles)
❸ Main Stand
❹ Popular Side

Left:
The Auto Windscreen Cup is one route by which lower division teams can savour the atmosphere of a final at Wembley. The 1996/97 final saw Colchester play Carlisle; unfortunately for United, Carlisle ran away with the cup. Here Carlisle's Will Varty and United's Paul Abrahams compete for the ball during the final.

COVENTRY CITY

Highfield Stadium, King Richard Street, Coventry CV2 4FW.

Tel No: 01203 234000
Advance Tickets Tel No: 01203 234020
Fax: 01203 234099
League: F.A. Premier
Brief History: Founded 1883 as Singers F.C., changed name to Coventry City in 1898. Former grounds; Dowell's Field, Stoke Road Ground, moved to Highfield Road in 1899. Record attendance, 51,455.
(Total) Current Capacity: 23,662 all seated
Visiting Supporters' Allocation: 4,154 all seated

Club Colours: Sky blue shirts, sky blue shorts.
Nearest Railway Station: Coventry.
Parking (Car): Street parking
Parking (Coach/Bus): Gosford Green Coach Park.
Police Force and Tel No: West Midlands (01203 539010)
Disabled Visitors' Facilities
   Wheelchairs: Clock Stand and East Stand
   Blind: Clock Stand (booking necessary)

KEY	
C	Club Offices
S	Club Shop
E	Entrance(s) for visiting supporters
R	Refreshment bars for visiting supporters
T	Toilets for visiting supporters

↑ North direction (approx)

❶ Swan Lane
❷ A4600 Walsgrave Road
❸ Thackhall Street
❹ Coventry BR Station (1 mile)
❺ To M6 Junction 2 and M69
❻ To M45 Junction 1
❼ Gosford Green Coach Park

Left:
One of the Premiership's eternal
strugglers, each season the pundits
reckon that Coventry will be
doomed to face the drop and yet the
team survives. The 1996/97 season
was no different, with Ron Atkinson
replaced as Team Manager by
Gordon Strachan early on and all
hanging on the results of games on
the final Sunday of the season. The
team, however, managed to evade
the drop yet again, with Coventry
winning at Tottenham and
Sunderland losing at Wimbledon;
Coventry's miraculous hold on top
flight football ensures Premiership
football for another year. One of the
team's recruits for 1996/97 was Gary
McAllister, who is seen in action in
the league game against
Nottingham Forest on 17 August
1996.

CREWE ALEXANDRA

Gresty Road Ground, Crewe, Cheshire, CW2 6EB

Tel No: 01270 213014
Advance Tickets Tel No: 01270 252610
Fax: 01270 216320
League: 1st Division
Brief History: Founded 1877. Former Grounds: Alexandra Recreation ground (Nantwich Road), Earle Street Cricket Ground, Edleston Road, Old Sheds Fields, Gresty Road (Adjacent to current Ground), moved to current Ground in 1906. Founder members of 2nd Division (1892) until 1896. Founder members of 3rd Division North (1921). Record attendance 20,000.

(Total) Current Capacity: 5,900 (4,800 seate
Visiting Supporters' Allocation: 972
Club Colours: Red Shirts, White Shorts.
Nearest Railway Station: Crewe.
Parking (Car): Car Park near Ground
Parking (Coach/Bus): Car Park near Ground
Police Force and Tel No: Cheshire (01270 500222)
Disabled Visitors' Facilities
   Wheelchairs: In visitors stand
   Blind: Commentary available

KEY

C Club Offices
S Club Shop
E Entrance(s) for visiting supporters
R Refreshment bars for visiting supporters
T Toilets for visiting supporters

↑ North direction (approx)

❶ Crewe BR Station
❷ Car Park
❸ Gresty Road
❹ A534 Nantwich Road
❺ A5020 to M6 Junction 16
❻ To M6 Junction 17

Left:
The widely admired manager of Crewe Alexandra, Dario Gradi, had finally the success that he merited when his skilful team overcame Brentford in the 2nd Division Play-Off Final at Wembley on 25 May 1997 to take the team, for the first time since 1896, back to the old 2nd (now 1st) Division.
Crewe's Dele Adebola avoids the sliding tackle of Brentford's Gus Hurdle and the attention of Jamie Bates during the all-important game at Wembley.

CRYSTAL PALACE

Selhurst Park, London, SE25 6PU

Tel No: 0181 768 6000
Advance Tickets Tel No: 0181 771 8841
Fax: 0181 768 6114
Ticket Office/Fax: 0181 653 4708
League: F.A. Premier
Brief History: Founded 1905. Former Grounds: The Crystal Palace (F.A. Cup Finals venue), London County Athletic Ground (Herne Hill), The Nest (Croydon Common Athletic Ground), moved to Selhurst Park in 1924. Founder members 3rd Division (1920). Record attendance 51,482.
(Total) Current Capacity: 26,400 all seated
Visiting Supporters' Allocation: Approx 2,500
Club Colours: Red with blue striped shirts, red shorts

Nearest Railway Station: Selhurst, Norwood Junction & Thornton Heath
Parking (Car): Street parking & Sainsbury's c park
Parking (Coach/Bus): Thornton Heath
Police Force and Tel No: Metropolitan (018 653 8568)
Disabled Visitors' Facilities
  Wheelchairs: Arthur Wait and Holmesdale Stands
  Blind: Commentary available
Anticipated Development(s): Planning permission has been obtained for the construction of a new Main Stand. As yet the is no confirmed start date.

KEY

C Club Offices
S Club Shop
E Entrance(s) for visiting supporters
T Toilets for visiting supporters

↑ North direction (approx)

❶ Whitehorse Lane
❷ Park Road
❸ A213 Selhurst Road
❹ Selhurst BR Station (1/2 mile)
❺ Norwood Junction BR Station (1/4 mile)
❻ Thornton Heath BR Station (1/2 mile)
❼ Car Park (Sainsbury's)

Left:
Now again under the astute management of Steve Coppell, following the departure of Dave Bassett, the Eagles soared to the Play-Offs for the second season in succession. This year, however, there was no repeat of the traumas experienced in the defeat by Leicester as Palace beat Sheffield United 1-0 to regain a place in English football's top flight. On 10 November 1996 Palace's Andy Roberts is pictured during the 1st Division match against fellow London team Queens Park Rangers.

DARLINGTON

Feethams Ground, Darlington, DL1 5JB

Tel No: 01325 465097
Advance Tickets Tel No: 01325 465097
Fax: 01325 381377
League: 3rd Division
Brief History: Founded 1883. Founder Members of 3rd Division North (1921), Relegated from 4th Division (1989). Promoted from GM Vauxhall Conference in 1990. Record attendance 21,023.
(Total) Current Capacity: 6,709 (1,120 seated)
Visiting Supporters' Allocation: 800 (200 seated)
Club Colours: White and Black Shirts, Black Shorts.

Nearest Railway Station: Darlington
Parking (Car): Street parking
Parking (Coach/Bus): As directed by Police
Police Force and Tel No: Durham (01325 467681)
Disabled Visitors' Facilities
　Wheelchairs: East Stand (free entrance)
　Blind: By prior arrangement
Anticipated Development(s): Work on the redevelopment of Feethams will start during summer of 1997. The first phase will see work on the East Stand and the Cricket Ground End. When completed the ground will have a capacity of 10,048.

KEY

C Club Offices
S Club Shop
E Entrance(s) for visiting supporters
R Refreshment bars for visiting supporters
T Toilets for visiting supporters

↑ North direction (approx)

❶ Polam Lane
❷ Victoria Embankment
❸ Feethams Cricket Ground
❹ Victoria Road
❺ Darlington BR Station (1/4 mile)
❻ To A1 (M)

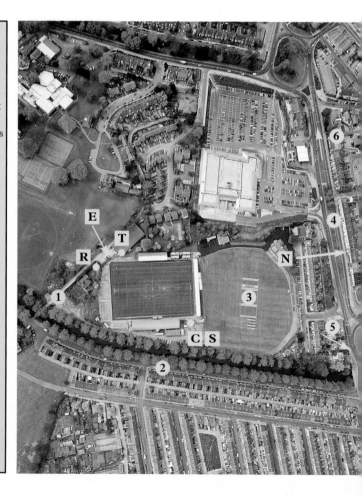

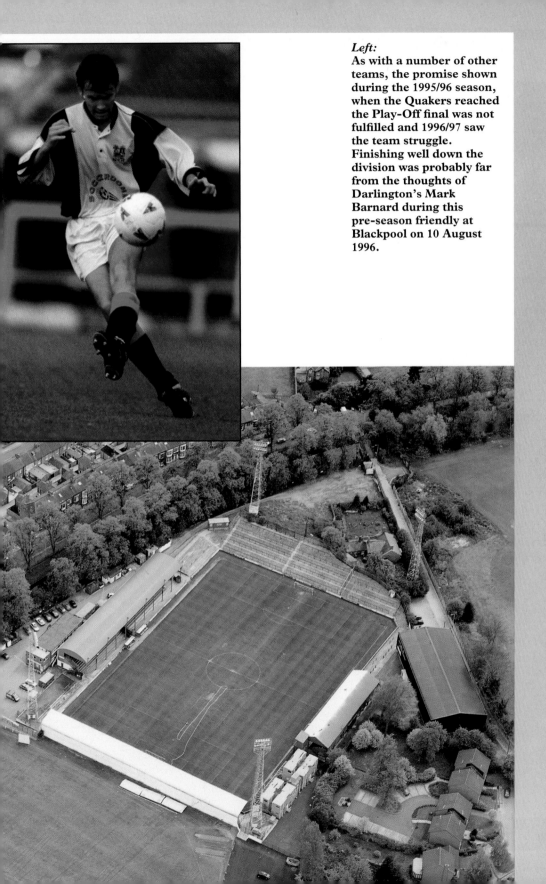

Left:
As with a number of other teams, the promise shown during the 1995/96 season, when the Quakers reached the Play-Off final was not fulfilled and 1996/97 saw the team struggle. Finishing well down the division was probably far from the thoughts of Darlington's Mark Barnard during this pre-season friendly at Blackpool on 10 August 1996.

DERBY COUNTY

Pride Park, Derby, Derbyshire

Tel No: 01332 340105★
Advance Tickets Tel No: 01332 340105★
Fax: 01332 293514★
★ Note these are the numbers for the Baseball Ground; at the time of writing it is unclear whether these will be transferred to the new ground.
League: F. A. Premiership
Brief History: Founded 1884. Former grounds: The Racecourse Ground, the Baseball Ground (1894-1997), moved to Pride Park 1997. Founder members of the Football League (1888). Record capacity at the Baseball Ground: 41,826.
(Total) Current Capacity: 30,139 (all seated)
Visiting Supporters' Allocation: 4,800 in the South Stand

Club Colours: White shirts and black shorts
Nearest Railway Station: Derby
Parking (Cars): 2,300 places at the ground designated for season ticket holders. Also two 1,000 car parks on the A6/A52 link road. No on-street parking.
Parking (Coach/Bus): As directed
Police Force and Tel No: Derbyshire (01332 290100)
Disabled Visitors' Facilities:
  Wheelchairs: 70 home/30 away spaces
  Blind: Commentary available
Anticipated Development(s): There are plans for the construction of wing-stands linking the North and South stands with the West Stand but nothing is confirmed at this stage.

KEY

⬆ North direction (approx)

❶ Derby Midland BR station
❷ North Stand
❸ West Stand
❹ South Stand (away)
❺ East Stand
❻ Link Road
❼ To A52/M1
❽ To City Centre and A6

Left:
One of the teams most heavily backed for an immediate return to the 1st Division, Jim Smith's Derby County retained their position in the top flight which will ensure that the first season at the club's new ground will see games against Liverpool and Manchester United rather than Bury and Stockport County. One factor in the Rams success back in the Premiership was the form of striker Dean Sturridge, pictured here in the home league game against Aston Villa on 12 April 1997.

DONCASTER ROVERS

Belle Vue, Bawtry Road, Doncaster DN4 5HT

Tel No: 01302 539441
Advance Tickets Tel No: 01302 539441
Fax: 01302 539679
League: 3rd Division
Brief History: Founded 1879. Former Grounds: Town Moor, Belle Vue (not current Ground), Deaf School Playing Field (later name Intake Ground), Bennetthorpe, moved to Belle Vue (former name Low Pasture) in 1922. Record attendance 37,099.
(Total) Current Capacity: 7,794 (1,259 seated)
Visiting Supporters' Allocation: 1,398 (194 seated)

Club Colours: Red Shirts and Shorts.
Nearest Railway Station: Doncaster
Parking (Car): Car Park at ground
Parking (Coach/Bus): Car Park at ground
Police Force and Tel No: South Yorkshire (01302 366744)
Disabled Visitors' Facilities
Wheelchairs: Bawtry Road
Blind: No special facility
Anticipated Development(s): The club hope to relocate to a new site but nothing has been confirmed.

KEY

C Club Offices
S Club Shop
E Entrance(s) for visiting supporters
R Refreshment bars for visiting supporters
T Toilets for visiting supporters

⬆ North direction (approx)

❶ A638 Bawtry Road
❷ Racecourse
❸ Car Park
❹ To Doncaster BR Station & A1(M) (3 miles)
❺ To A630 & M18 Junction 4

EVERTON

Goodison Park, Goodison Road, Liverpool, L4 4EL

Tel No: 0151 330 2200
Advance Tickets Tel No: 0151 330 2300
Fax: 0151 286 9112
League: FA Premier
Brief History: Founded 1879 as St. Domingo, changed to Everton in 1880. Former Grounds: Stanley Park, Priory Road and Anfield (Liverpool F.C. Ground), moved to Goodison Park in 1892. Founder-members Football League (1888). Record attendance 78,229.
(Total) Current Capacity: 40,200 all seated
Visiting Supporters' Allocation: 2,669
Club Colours: Blue shirts, white shorts

Nearest Railway Station: Liverpool Lime Str
Parking (Car): Corner of Utting & Priory Avenues
Parking (Coach/Bus): Priory Road
Police Force and Tel No: Merseyside (0151 709 6010)
Disabled Visitors' Facilities
Wheelchairs: Bullens Road Stand.
Blind: Commentary available
Anticipated Development(s): Following a vo in favour by the supporters, it is likely that th club will move to a new stadium with a capac of 60,000.

KEY

C Club Offices
S Club Shop
E Entrance(s) for visiting supporters
R Refreshment bars for visiting supporters
T Toilets for visiting supporters

↑ North direction (approx)

❶ A580 Walton Road
❷ Bullens Road
❸ Goodison Road
❹ Car Park
❺ Liverpool Lime Street BR Station (2 miles)
❻ To M57 Junction 2, 4 and 5
❼ Stanley Park

Right:

Another high profile managerial casualty in the Premiership during the 96/97 season was the departure of Joe Royle from Everton. A team that promised much failed to deliver and it will be interesting to see what the new manager, Howard Kendall, will make of Duncan Ferguson and the rest of the team. Everton's powerful striker makes contact with the ball during the home game against Middlesbrough on 7 September 1996.

EXETER CITY

St. James Park, Exeter, EX4 6PX

Tel No: 01392 254073
Advance Tickets Tel No: 01392 254073
Fax: 01392 425885
League: 3rd Division
Brief History: Founded in 1904. (From amalgamation of St. Sidwell United and Exeter United.) Founder-members Third Division (1920). Record attendance 20,984.
(Total) Current Capacity: 10,570 (1,690 seated)
Visiting Supporters' Allocation: 1,274
Club Colours: Red and white striped shirts, black shorts
Nearest Railway Station: Exeter St. James Park

Parking (Car): National Car Park and Counc Car Parks (No street parking)
Parking (Coach/Bus): Paris Street bus statio
Police Force and Tel No: Devon and Cornw (01392 52101)
Disabled Visitors' Facilities
   Wheelchairs: St. James Road entrance (pri booking)
   Blind: No special facility
Anticipated Development(s): Now that the club's position is more secure and the groun has been acquired by the local council, there are plans to rebuild St James' Park. Work wi probably start in 1998 and will involve the St James Road End initially.

KEY

C Club Offices
S Club Shop
E Entrance(s) for visiting supporters
T Toilets for visiting supporters

↑ North direction (approx)

❶ Exeter St. James Park BR Station
❷ St. James Road
❸ Old Tiverton Road
❹ Blackboy Road

ght:

rtunately for Exeter
ere was at least one team
the 3rd Division worse
an the Grecians,
herwise City would have
en facing the likelihood
Conference fixtures
ainst, for example,
uthport and Rushden &
amonds. That dubious
te, however, befell
reford United and
xeter can look forward to
e new season travelling to
miliar haunts. City's
rry McConnell is caught
ring a pre-season
endly against high-
ending Chelsea on
July 1996.

FULHAM

Craven Cottage, Stevenage Road, Fulham, London, SW6 6HH

Tel No: 0171 736 6561
Advance Tickets Tel No: 0171 736 6561
Fax: 0171 731 7047
League: 2nd Division
Brief History: Founded in 1879 as St. Andrews Fulham, changed name to Fulham in 1898. Former Grounds: Star Road, Ranelagh Club, Lillie Road, Eel Brook Common, Purser's Cross, Barn Elms and Half Moon (Wasps Rugby Football Ground), moved to Craven Cottage in 1894. Record attendance 49,335.
(Total) Current Capacity: 14,969 (5,119 seated)
Visiting Supporters' Allocation: approx 2,400
Club Colours: White shirts, black shorts
Nearest Railway Station: Putney Bridge (Tube)
Parking (Car): Street parking
Parking (Coach/Bus): Stevenage Road

Police Force and Tel No: Metropolitan (0171 741 6212)
Disabled Visitors' Facilities
  Wheelchairs: Main Stand
  Blind: No special facility
Anticipated Development(s): The club has now secured the freehold of Craven Cottage and is looking to redevelop. Much of the ground is listed — which will obviously constrain some work — and the club has recently been acquired by Mohamed al-Fayed, the owner of Harrods, following the retirement of Jimmy Hill. Plans envisage the conversion the stadium into a 15,000 all-seater affair. Initial work started in June 1997 on the dressing rooms. The away fans' allocation in the Riverside Stand has been ended due to development work.

KEY
- **C** Club Offices (The Cottage)
- **S** Club Shop
- **E** Entrance(s) for visiting supporters
- **R** Refreshment bars for visiting supporters
- **T** Toilets for visiting supporters

↑ North direction (approx)

❶ River Thames
❷ Stevenage Road
❸ Finlay Street
❹ Putney Bridge Tube Station (1/2 mile)

Left:
A new season and a new owner; the 1997/98 promises to be an interesting one for Fulham supporters. Coming second in the 3rd Division brings 2nd Division football to Craven Cottage, whilst the retirement of Jimmy Hill and the acquisition of the club by Harrods' owner Mohamed al-Fayed suggests that money will be available for ground and team rebuilding. It will be interesting to see how long Fulham's links with the GMB trade union — as evinced by Mike Conroy's shirt — will survive in the new era.

GILLINGHAM

Priestfield Stadium, Redfern Avenue, Gillingham, Kent, ME7 4DD

Tel No: 01634 851854
Advance Tickets Tel No: 01634 576828
Fax: 01634 850986
League: 2nd Division
Brief History: Founded 1893, as New Brompton, changed name to Gillingham in 1913. Founder-members Third Division (1920). Lost Football League status (1938), re-elected to Third Division South (1950). Record attendance 23,002.
(Total) Current Capacity: 12,722 (3,525 seated)
Visiting Supporters' Allocation: 1,900

Club Colours: Blue shirts, blue shorts
Nearest Railway Station: Gillingham
Parking (Car): Street parking
Parking (Coach/Bus): As directed by Police
Police Force and Tel No: Kent (01634 8344⦁
Disabled Visitors' Facilities
   Wheelchairs: Redfern Avenue
   Blind: No special facility
Anticipated Development(s): Although there still the long-term possibility of relocation, the recent completion of the redevelopment of the Gordon Street stand suggests that the club w stay at Priestfield at least in the medium term

KEY

C Club Offices
S Club Shop
E Entrance(s) for visiting supporters
R Refreshment bars for visiting supporters
T Toilets for visiting supporters

⬆ North direction (approx)

❶ Redfern Avenue
❷ Toronto Road
❸ Gordon Road
❹ Gillingham BR Station (¼ mile)
❺ Woodlands Road

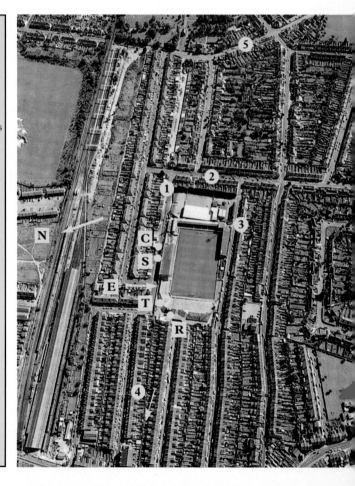

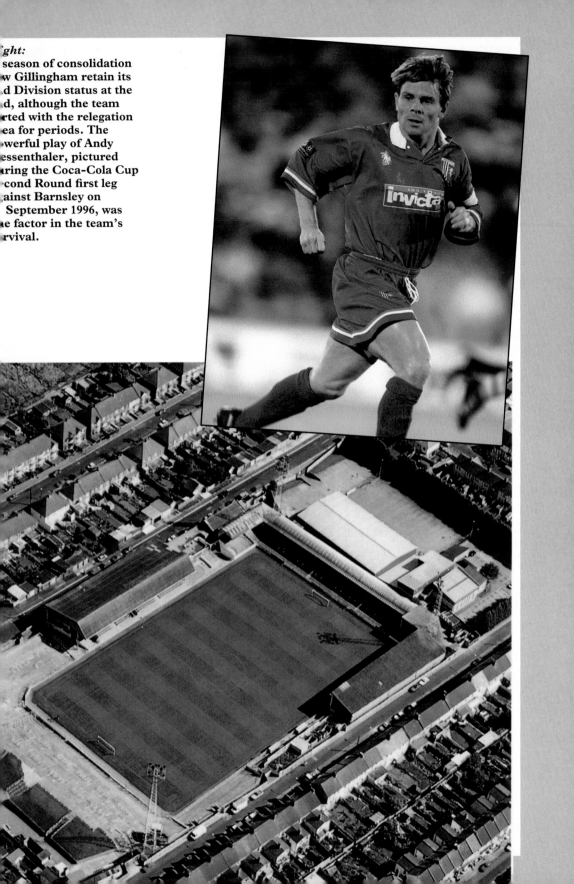

Right:
... season of consolidation
... Gillingham retain its
... Division status at the
..., although the team
...ted with the relegation
...ea for periods. The
...werful play of Andy
...essenthaler, pictured
...ring the Coca-Cola Cup
...cond Round first leg
...ainst Barnsley on
... September 1996, was
...e factor in the team's
...rvival.

GRIMSBY TOWN

Blundell Park, Cleethorpes, DN35 7PY

Tel No: 01472 697111
Advance Tickets Tel No: 01472 697111
Fax: 01472 693665
League: 2nd Division
Brief History: Founded 1878, as Grimsby
Pelham, changed name to Grimsby Town in
1879. Former Grounds: Clee Park (two
adjacent fields) & Abbey Park, moved to
Blundell Park in 1899. Founder-members 2nd
Division (1892). Record attendance 31,651.
(Total) Current Capacity: 8,870 (all seated)

Visiting Supporters' Allocation: 1,874
Club Colours: Black & white striped shirts, bla
shorts
Nearest Railway Station: Cleethorpes
Parking (Car): Street Parking
Parking (Coach/Bus): Harrington Street
Police Force and Tel No: Humberside (0147
359171)
Disabled Visitors' Facilities
Wheelchairs: Harrington Street
Blind: Commentary available

KEY
C Club Offices (Findus Stand)
S Club Shop
E Entrance(s) for visiting
supporters
R Refreshment bars for visiting
supporters
T Toilets for visiting supporters

↑ North direction (approx)

❶ A180 Grimsby Road
❷ Cleethorpes BR Station
(1¹/₂ miles)
❸ To Grimsby and M180
Junction 5
❹ Harrington Street
❺ Constitutional Avenue
❻ Humber Estuary

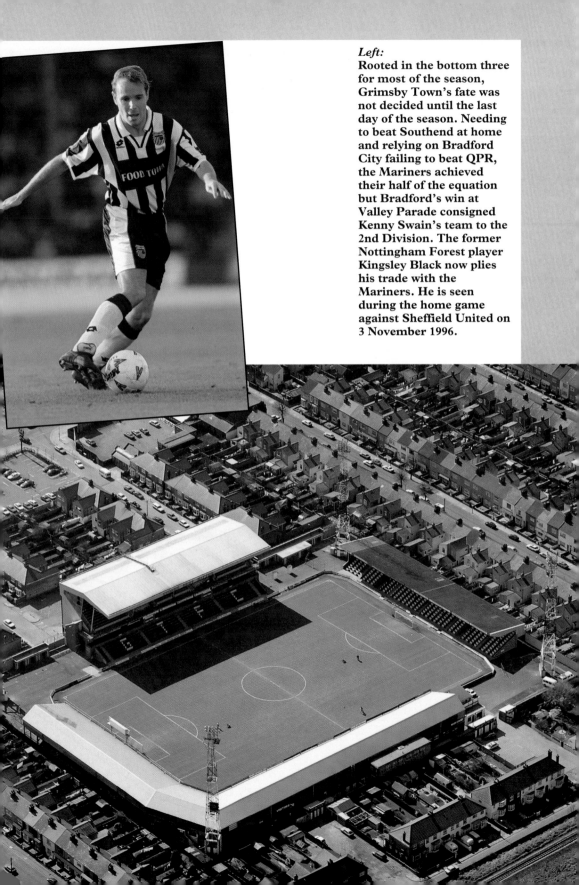

Left:

Rooted in the bottom three for most of the season, Grimsby Town's fate was not decided until the last day of the season. Needing to beat Southend at home and relying on Bradford City failing to beat QPR, the Mariners achieved their half of the equation but Bradford's win at Valley Parade consigned Kenny Swain's team to the 2nd Division. The former Nottingham Forest player Kingsley Black now plies his trade with the Mariners. He is seen during the home game against Sheffield United on 3 November 1996.

HARTLEPOOL UNITED

Victoria Ground, Clarence Road, Hartlepool, TS24 8BZ

Tel No: 01429 272584
Advance Tickets Tel No: 01429 272584
Fax: 01429 863007
League: 3rd Division
Brief History: Founded 1908 as Hartlepools United, changed to Hartlepool (1968) and to Hartlepool United in 1977. Founder-members 3rd Division (1921). Record attendance 17,426.
(Total) Current Capacity: 7,271 (4,008 seated)
Visiting Supporters' Allocation: 741 (located in Rink Stand)
Club Colours: Blue & white striped shirts, Blue shorts
Nearest Railway Station: Hartlepool Church Street

Parking (car): Street parking and rear of clock garage
Police Force and Tel No: Cleveland (01429 221151)
Disabled Visitors' Facilities
  Wheelchairs: Cyril Knowles Stand
  Blind: Commentary available
Anticipated Development(s): Work is likely affect the Millhouse Stand side with the construction of a Conference and Leisure Centre during the 1997/98 season. As a resul season tickets for this section of the ground a not being sold.

KEY

C Club Offices
S Club Shop
E Entrance(s) for visiting supporters

⬆ North direction (approx)

❶ A1088 Clarence Road
❷ Hartlepool Church Street BR Station
❸ A179 Raby Road
❹ Greyhound Stadium
❺ To Middlesbrough A689 & A1(M)

Right:

Now approaching their 90th anniversary, Hartlepool United will again be featuring in the 3rd Division programme. The 1996/97 season saw the team in the lower half of the table and with the leading Vauxhall Conference clubs now ensuring that their grounds are up to scratch — plus the possibility of increased relegation-promoted between the 3rd and the GMVC — United fans will be hoping for an improved performance from the team. Stephen Howard makes his point during the game with Hereford United in April 1996.

HUDDERSFIELD TOWN

The Alfred McAlpine Stadium, Leeds Road, Huddersfield, HD1 6P

Tel No: 01484 420335
Advance Tickets Tel No: 01484 424444
Fax: 01484 515122
League: 1st Division
Brief History: Founded 1908, elected to Football League in 1910. First Club to win the Football League Championship three years in succession. Moved from Leeds Road ground to Kirklees (Alfred McAlpine) Stadium 1994/95 season. Record attendance (Leeds Road) 67,037.
(Total) Current Capacity: 19,600 (all seated)
Visiting Supporters' Allocation: 4,053 (all seated)
Club Colours: Blue and white striped shirts, white shorts

Nearest Railway Station: Huddersfield
Parking (Car): Car parks adjacent to ground
Parking (Coach/Bus): Car parks adjacent to ground
Police Force and Tel No: West Yorkshire (01484 422122)
Disabled Visitors' Facilities
 Wheelchairs: Three sides of Ground, at low levels and raised areas, including toilets acce
 Blind: Area for Partially sighted with Hospi Radio commentary.
Anticipated Development(s): Work has now started on the fourth stand at the McAlpine Stadium, which will take the ground's capaci to 25,000. Estimated completion date will al its use from the start of the 1998/99 season.

KEY

C Club Offices
S Club Shop
E Entrance(s) for visiting supporters
R Refreshment bars for visiting supporters
T Toilets for visiting supporters

↑ North direction (approx)

❶ To Leeds and M62 Junction 25
❷ A62 Leeds Road
❸ To Huddersfield BR station (1¼ miles)
❹ Disabled parking
❺ Town Avenue pay car park (on site of former ground)
❻ North Stand (under construction)
❼ St Andrews pay car park
❽ Coach park

ght:
though Huddersfield had
allenged for a Play-Off
ot at the end of the 1995/96
ason, the Terriers second
ason back in the 1st
ivision proved more of a
ruggle and the team found
elf just above the
legation spots at the end of
e season. Jon Dyson is
ctured in the league match
ainst Wolves at the Alfred
cAlpine stadium on 8
bruary 1997.

HULL CITY

Boothferry Park, Boothferry Road, Hull, HU4 6EU

Tel No: 01482 351119
Advance Tickets Tel No: 01482 351119
Fax: 01482 565752
League: 3rd Division
Brief History: Founded 1904. Former grounds: The Boulevard (Hull Rugby League Ground), Dairycoates, Anlaby Road Cricket Circle (Hull Cricket Ground), Anlaby Road, moved to Boothferry Park in 1946. Record attendance 55,019.
(Total) Current Capacity: 12,996 (5,495 seated)
Visiting Supporters' Allocation: 2,090 (530 seated)
Club Colours: Amber shirts, black shorts
Nearest Railway Station: Hull Paragon

Parking (Car): Street Parking and at ground (limited)
Parking (Coach/Bus): At ground
Police Force and Tel No: Humberside (0148 220148)
Disabled Visitors' Facilities
  Wheelchairs: Corner East/South stands
  Blind: Commentary available
Anticipated Development(s): Given the club financial problems, the planned East Stand is unlikely to proceed. The club has now been taken over by a consortium that also controls Hull Sharks Rugby League team. It is planned that the football club will move to the RLFC ground during the 1997/98 season.

KEY
C Club Offices
E Entrance(s) for visiting supporters

↑ North direction (approx)

❶ A63 Boothferry Road
❷ North Road
❸ Hull Paragon BR Station (1½ miles)
❹ To Humber Bridge and M62 Junction 38

Left:
Following City's relegation
at the end of the 1995/96
season, the team struggled
in the 3rd Division and
ended up in a poor 17th
position. The take-over by
a new consortium, which
has also gained control of
Hull Sharks RLFC, along
with the dismissal of Terry
Dolan as manager, means
that the 1997/98 season will
be one of great change for
the club, both on and off
the pitch(es). Jimmy
Graham restarts the action
in this game from early
1996.

IPSWICH TOWN

Portman Road, Ipswich, IP1 2DA

Tel No: 01473 400500
Advance Tickets Tel No: 01473 400555
Fax: 01473 400040
League: 1st Division
Brief History: Founded 1887 as Ipswich
  Association F.C., changed to Ipswich Town in
  1888. Former Grounds: Broom Hill & Brookes
  Hall, moved to Portman Road in 1888. Record
  attendance 38,010
(Total) Current Capacity: 22,500 all seated
Visiting Supporters Allocation: 2,419 all
  seated

Club Colours: Blue shirts, white shorts
Nearest Railway Station: Ipswich
Parking (Car): Portman Road, Portman Walk
  West End Road
Parking (Coach/Bus): West End Road
Police Force and Tel No: Suffolk (01473
  611611)
Disabled Visitors' Facilities
  Wheelchairs: Lower Pioneer Stand
  Blind: Commentary available

KEY

C Club Offices
S Club Shop
E Entrance(s) for visiting
  supporters
R Refreshment bars for visiting
  supporters
T Toilets for visiting supporters

↑ North direction (approx)

❶ A137 West End Road
❷ Portman Walk
❸ Portman Road
❹ Princes Street
❺ Ipswich BR Station
❻ Car Parks

Left:
The nearly men of 1995/96 went one better at the end of 1996/97 and reached the 1st Division Play-Offs. No doubt the team's success was made all the more sweet by the fact that amongst the teams pipped for this were local rivals Norwich City; however, Sheffield United were to beat Town over the two legs on the away goals rule. In the FA Cup, Town came up against Nottingham Forest at the City Ground on 4 January 1997 and Jason Cundy is seen during the game.

LEEDS UNITED

Elland Road, Leeds, LS11 0ES

Tel No: 0113 226 6000
Advance Tickets Tel No: 0113 226 1000
Fax: 0113 226 6050
League: F.A. Premier
Brief History: Founded 1919, formed from the former 'Leeds City' Club, who were disbanded following expulsion from the Football League in October 1919. Joined Football League in 1920. Record attendance 57,892
(Total) Current Capacity: 40,000 (all seated)
Visiting Supporters' Allocation: 1,850 in South East Corner (can be increased to 3,950 in South Stand if necessary)

Club Colours: White shirts, white shorts
Nearest Railway Station: Leeds City
Parking (Car): Car parks adjacent to ground
Parking (Coach/Bus): As directed by Police
Police Force and Tel No: West Yorkshire (01 243 5353)
Disabled Visitors' Facilities
  Wheelchairs: West Stand and South Stand
  Blind: Commentary available

KEY

C Club Offices
S Club Shop
E Entrance(s) for visiting supporters

↑ North direction (approx)

❶ M621
❷ M621 Junction 2
❸ A643 Elland Road
❹ Lowfields Road
❺ To A58
❻ City Centre and BR station
❼ To M62 and M1

Right:
Now managed by George Graham, rehabilitated after his departure from Arsenal following allegations linking him with a Scandinavian agent, Leeds United — despite several high profile signings — achieved little other than being the butt of a joke in an advert for a mobile phone ('Leeds United 0 Rotherham 3'). One of many players that found it difficult to sustain his scoring record was veteran ex-Liverpool striker Ian Rush, pictured here in the Premiership game against local rivals Sheffield Wednesday on 20 August 1996.

LEICESTER CITY

City Stadium, Filbert Street, Leicester, LE2 7FL

Tel No: 0116 291 5000
Advance Tickets Tel No: 0116 291 5232
Fax: 0116 247 0585
League: F.A. Premier
Brief History: Founded 1884 as Leicester Fosse, changed name to Leicester City in 1919. Former Grounds: Fosse Road South, Victoria Road, Belgrave Cycle Track, Mill Lane & Aylestone Road Cricket Ground, moved to Filbert Street in 1891. Record attendance 47,298
(Total) Current Capacity: 21,500 (all seated)

Visiting Supporters' Allocation: 1,866 in East Stand Blocks T and U
Club Colours: Blue shirts, white shorts
Nearest Railway Station: Leicester
Parking (Car): NCP car park & street parking
Parking (Coach/Bus): Western Boulevard
Police Force and Tel No: Leicester (0116 253 0066)
Disabled Visitors' Facilities
  Wheelchairs: Filbert Street
  Blind: Commentary available (from August 1997)

KEY

C Club Offices
S Club Shop
E Entrance(s) for visiting supporters
R Refreshment bars for visiting supporters
T Toilets for visiting supporters

↑ North direction (approx)

❶ Walnut Street
❷ Filbert Street
❸ Grasmere Street
❹ River Soar
❺ M1 and M69 Junction 21
❻ Leicester BR Station (1 mile)

LEYTON ORIENT

Leyton Stadium, Brisbane Road, Leyton, London, E10 5NE

Tel No: 0181 539 2223
Advance Tickets Tel No: 0181 539 2223
Fax: 0181 539 4390
E-Mail: orient@matchroom.com
League: 3rd Division
Brief History: Founded 1887 as Clapton Orient, from Eagle Cricket Club (formerly Glyn Cricket Club formed in 1881). Changed name to Leyton Orient (1946), Orient (1966), Leyton Orient (1987). Former grounds: Glyn Road, Whittles Athletic Ground, Millfields Road, Lea Bridge Road, Wembley Stadium (2 games), moved to Brisbane Road in 1937. Record attendance 34,345.
(Total) Current Capacity: 13,842 (7,133 seated)
Visiting Supporters' Allocation: 2,177
Club Colours: Red and white shirts, black shorts

Nearest Railway Station: Leyton (tube), Leyton Midland Road
Parking (Car): Street parking
Parking (Coach/Bus): As directed by Police
Police Force and Tel No: Metropolitan (0181 556 8855)
Disabled Visitors Facilities
　Wheelchairs: Windsor Road
　Blind: Match commentary supplied on request
Anticipated Development(s): The original South End was demolished in 1996 and the site is temporarily used as a car park. It is planned to have a new 3,000-seat stand open on the site by May 1998. This will be the first phase of a scheme to redevelop the ground completely, which will, inter alia, involve the pitch being rotated by 90°.

KEY

C Club Offices
S Club Shop
E Entrance(s) for visiting supporters

↑ North direction (approx)

❶ Buckingham Road
❷ Oliver Road
❸ A112 High Road Leyton
❹ Leyton Tube Station (1/4 mile)
❺ Brisbane Road
❻ Windsor Road
❼ Leyton Midland Road BR station
❽ South Stand (to be built)

Left:
Now chaired by sports promoter Barrie Hearn and with snooker player Steve Davis as a board member, you'd think that Orient would be good at slotting balls into nets. Unfortunately, a mid-table position perhaps indicates that the team's talents lie elsewhere. Russell Terry seems to have all the time in the world in this 3rd Division class with Cambridge United on 4 May 1996.

LINCOLN CITY

Sincil Bank, Lincoln, LN5 8LD

Tel No: 01522 880011
Advance Tickets Tel No: 01522 880011
Fax: 01522 880020
League: 3rd Division
Brief History: Founded 1884. Former Ground: John O'Gaunts Ground, moved to Sincil Bank in 1895. Founder-members 2nd Division Football League (1892). Relegated from 4th Division in 1987, promoted from GM Vauxhall Conference in 1988. Record attendance 23,196.
(Total) Current Capacity: 10,918 (9,246 seated)

Visiting Supporters' Allocation: 2,425 (all seated)
Club Colours: Red with white stripes shirts, white shorts
Nearest Railway Station: Lincoln Central
Parking (Car): Adjacent Ground
Parking (Coach/Bus): South Common
Police Force and Tel No: Lincolnshire (0152: 529911)
Disabled Visitors' Facilities
  Wheelchairs: Linpave and South Park stand
  Blind: No special facility

KEY

C Club Offices
S Club Shop
E Entrance(s) for visiting supporters
R Refreshment bars for visiting supporters
T Toilets for visiting supporters

⬆ North direction (approx)

❶ A46 High Street
❷ Sincil Bank
❸ Sausthorpe Street
❹ Cross Street
❺ A158 Canwick Road
❻ A158 South Park Avenue
❼ Car Park
❽ Lincoln Central BR Station (1/2 mile)

Left:
Whilst City may not have had the most successful of seasons in the 3rd Division, the team could claim to having one achieved one major surprise during the season — the defeat of Manchester City in the Coca-Cola Cup; but then, given Manchester City's dismal start to the 1996/97 season perhaps the Imps' victory was not all that surprising. Here Terry Flemming of Lincoln battles with Manchester's Nicky Summerbee during the first leg game at Sincil Bank on 17 September 1996.

LIVERPOOL

Anfield Road, Liverpool, L4 0TH

Tel No: 0151 263 2361
Advance Tickets Tel No: 0151 260 8680/
  0151 260 9999
Fax: 0151 260 8813
League: F.A. Premier
Brief History: Founded 1892. Anfield Ground
  formerly Everton F.C. Ground. Joined Football
  League in 1893. Record attendance 61,905.
(Total) Current Capacity: Approx 37,000 (all
  seated)
Visiting Supporters' Allocation: Nil for
  1997/98
Club Colours: Red shirts, red shorts
Nearest Railway Station: Kirkdale
Parking (Car): Stanley car park

Parking (Coach/Bus): Priory Road & Pinehu:
  Avenue
Police Force and Tel No: Merseyside (0151
  709 6010)
Disabled Visitors' Facilities
  Wheelchairs: Kop and Main Stands
  Blind: Commentary available
Anticipated Development(s): Work has
  started on the rebuilding of the Anfield Road
  Stand to increase its capacity to 8,000 and ta
  Anfield's total to more than 45,000. It is hop
  that part of the new stand will be open durin;
  1997/98 but until it is Anfield will be restricte
  to home fans only.

KEY
C Club Offices
S Club Shop

↑ North direction (approx)

❶ Car Park
❷ Anfield Road
❸ A5089 Walton Breck Road
❹ Kemlyn Road
❺ Kirkdale BR Station (1 mile)
❻ Utting Avenue
❼ Stanley Park
❽ Spion Kop

Right:
The 1996/97 season was a bit like the proverbial curate's egg for Liverpool. Reaching the semi-final of the Cup Winners Cup, a lamentable performance in Paris saw the Reds facing an uphill task in the return leg at Anfield — and yet the team almost managed the impossible by winning 2-0. In the Premiership, Liverpool's form was too erratic to maintain a challenge for the title. Much of Liverpool's success continues to be built upon the young shoulders of Robbie Fowler, whose goalscoring prowess is such that he broke the club's record for the fastest player to 100 goals during the season.

LUTON TOWN

Kenilworth Road Stadium, 1 Maple Road, Luton, LU4 8AW

Tel No: 01582 411622
Advance Tickets Tel No: 01582 416976
Fax: 01582 405070
League: 2nd Division
Brief History: Founded 1885 from an amalgamation of Wanderers F.C. & Excelsior F.C. Former Grounds: Dallow Lane & Dunstable Road, moved to Kenilworth Road in 1905. Record attendance 30,069.
(Total) Current Capacity: 9,975 (all seated)
Visiting Supporters' Allocation: 2,257
Club Colours: White with blue shoulder shirts, blue shorts with white side panel
Nearest Railway Station: Luton

Parking (Car): Street parking
Parking (Coach/Bus): Luton bus station
Police Force and Tel No: Bedfordshire (0158 401212)
Disabled Visitors' Facilities
  Wheelchairs: Kenilworth Road
  Blind: Commentary available
Anticipated Development(s): The future location of the club remains uncertain, with t lease on Kenilworth Road near the end of its term. The proposed 20,000 indoor stadium near Junction 10 of the M1 has been stalled and, if this does not proceed, the club is look at other locations, including Milton Keynes.

KEY

C Club Offices
S Club Shop
E Entrance(s) for visiting supporters
R Refreshment bars for visiting supporters
T Toilets for visiting supporters

↑ North direction (approx)

❶ To M1 Junction 11
❷ Wimborne Road
❸ Kenilworth Road
❹ Oak Road
❺ Dunstable Road
❻ Luton BR Station (1 mile)
❼ Ticket Office

96

Left:
Luton Town's first season back in the 2nd Division was reasonably successful, with the team, now managed by Lennie Lawrence, finishing third. However, defeat in the Play-Off semi-final against Crewe Alexandra consigned the Hatters to another season of 2nd Division football. Town's Liam George is pictured during a reserve team match against Arsenal on 3 October 1996; it is strange to think that it is not many years since the clubs' first teams would have met in a similar fixture.

MACCLESFIELD TOWN

Moss Rose Ground, London Road, Macclesfield, SK11 7SP

Tel No: 01625 264686
Advance Tickets Tel No: 01625 264686
Fax: 01625 264692
League: 3rd Division
Brief History: Founded 1874. Previous ground: Rostron Field moved to the Moss Rose Ground in 1891. Winners of the Vauxhall Conference in 1994/95 and 1996/97. Admitted to the Football League for 1997/98 season. Record attendance 9,003.
(Total) Current Capacity: 6,028 (1,053 seated)
Visiting Supporters' Allocation: 1,070 (Estate Road Terrace and Corner Paddock)
Club Colours: Blue shirts, white shorts
Nearest Railway Station: Macclesfield

Parking (Cars): No parking at the ground and the nearest off-street car park is in the town centre (25min walk). There is some on-street parking in the vicinity, but this can get crowded.
Parking (Coach/Bus): A directed
Police Force and Tel No: Cheshire (01625 610000)
Disabled Visitors' Facilities:
  Wheelchairs: Limited facilities
  Blind: No special facility
Anticipated Development(s): There are no definite plans for redevelopment although wo will need to be undertaken in due course.

KEY
C Club Offices
E Entrance(s) for visiting supporters

↑ North direction (approx)

❶ A523 London Road
❷ To Town Centre and BR station (1.5 miles)
❸ To Leek
❹ Moss Lane
❺ Star Lane
❻ Silkmans Public House
❼ Star Lane Stand
❽ Silkman End
❾ Estate Road Terrace (away section)

Left:

Following the disappointment of winning the Vauxhall Conference in 1994/95 but being refused admission to the 3rd Division as a result of their ground not fulfilling league criteria, Macclesfield Town achieved Nationwide League status as a result of their triumph in a tightly-fought Vauxhall Conference in 1996/97. Town's club captain Neil Howarth is pictured in action against Manchester United reserves on 17 August 1996.

MANCHESTER CITY

Maine Road, Moss Side, Manchester, M14 7WN

Tel No: 0161 224 5000
Advance Tickets Tel No: 0161 226 2224
Fax: 0161 248 8449
E-Mail: citynet@www.mcfc.co.uk
League: 1st Division
Brief History: Founded 1880 as West Gorton, changed name to Ardwick (reformed 1887) and to Manchester City in 1894. Former grounds: Clowes Street, Kirkmanshulme Cricket Club, Donkey Common, Pink Bank Lane & Hyde Road, moved to Maine Road in 1923. Founder-members 2nd Division (1892). Record attendance 84,569 (record for Football League ground).
(Total) Current Capacity: 32,146 (all seated)
Visiting Supporters' Allocation: 2,433
Club Colours: Sky blue shirts, white shorts

Nearest Railway Station: Manchester Piccadi (2½ miles)
Parking (Car): Street parking & local schools
Parking (Coach/Bus): Kippax Street car park
Police Force and Tel No: Greater Mancheste (0161 872 5050)
Disabled Visitors' Facilities
Wheelchairs: Umbro Stand / Kippax Stand
Blind: Main Stand 'G' Block
Anticipated Development(s): Long-term plar envisage expanding Maine Road to a 45,000-seater, but nothing is definitely planned at thi stage following City's relegation to the 1st Division at the end of the 1995/96 season. Previous plans for the construction of a linkin stand between the North and Kippax stands have been put on hold.

KEY
C Club Offices
S Club Shop
E Entrance(s) for visiting supporters

↑ North direction (approx)

❶ Thornton Road
❷ South Upper Lloyd Street
❸ To A5103 Princess Road
❹ To City Centre and Manchester Piccadilly BR Station (2½ miles)
❺ To A6010 & M31 Junction 7
❻ Maine Road
❼ Kippax Stand
❽ Main Stand
❾ Umbro Stand

Left:
A year of contrasting fortunes for Manchester's 'Big Two' clubs: Manchester United triumphant again in the Premiership whilst City had a disastrous start to the season slumming it in the 1st. At one time the team seemed to be going through managers faster than Shane Warne skittling out England's cricketers, but the appointment of ex-Forest boss Frank Clark brought stability and the team rose through the table. City's expensive squad will be expected to do a great deal better in 1997/98 and challenge for automatic promotion. Georgian star Georgiou Kinkladze, who could hardly have been expecting to play such teams as Southend and Grimsby when he signed for City, is pictured in the league game against Ipswich on 16 August 1996.

MANCHESTER UNITED

Old Trafford, Sir Matt Busby Way, Manchester, M16 0RA

Tel No: 0161 872 1661
Advance Tickets Tel No: 0161 872 0199
Fax: 0161 876 5502
League: F.A. Premier
Brief History: Founded in 1878 as 'Newton Heath L & Y', later Newton Heath, changed to Manchester United in 1902. Former Grounds: North Road, Monsall & Bank Street, Clayton, moved to Old Trafford in 1910 (used Manchester City F.C. Ground 1941-49). Founder-members Second Division (1892). Record attendance 76,962.
(Total) Current Capacity: 55,300 (all seated).
Visiting Supporters' Allocation: Approx. 3,000

Club Colours: Red shirts, white shorts
Nearest Railway Station: At Ground
Parking (Car): Lancashire Cricket Ground & White City
Parking (Coach/Bus): As directed by Police
Police Force and Tel No: Greater Manchester (0161 872 5050)
Disabled Visitors' Facilities
  Wheelchairs: South East Stand.
  Blind: Commentary available
Anticipated Development(s): With the completion of the North Stand nothing definit is planned.

KEY
C Club Offices
S Club Shops

↑ North direction (approx)

❶ To A5081 Trafford Park Road to M63 Junction 4 (5 miles)
❷ A56 Chester Road
❸ Manchester Ship Canal
❹ To Old Trafford Cricket Ground
❺ To Parking and Warwick Road BR Station
❻ Sir Matt Busby Way

Right:
Triumphant at home, but still awaiting European glory, Manchester United remain the team to beat in domestic competition. The club's fifth Championship in six years was not as cut and dried as in previous years — both Arsenal and Liverpool threatened to the end — but Alex Ferguson's team always looked capable of retaining their crown. It was a season, however, of contrasting form for Eric Cantona (now retired) and David Beckham; for the former the old magic seemed to have disappeared for much of the season whilst for the latter, the scoring of stunning goals seems to have become second nature. Here the duo are celebrating Beckham's winning goal in the fiercely contested match in the game against Liverpool on 12 October 1996.

MANSFIELD TOWN

Field Mill Ground, Quarry Lane, Mansfield, Notts, NG18 5DA

Tel No: 01623 23567
Advance Tickets Tel No: 01623 23567
Fax: 01623 25014
League: 3rd Division
Brief History: Founded 1910 as Mansfield Wesleyans Boys Brigade, changed to Mansfield Town in 1914. Former Grounds: Pelham Street, Newgate Lane & The Prairie, moved to Field Mill in 1919. Record attendance 24,467.
(Total) Current Capacity: 6,905 (2,695 seated)
Visiting Supporters' Allocation: 2,027 (563 seated)
Club Colours: Amber with blue trim shirts, Amber shorts with blue trim.

Nearest Railway Station: Mansfield
Parking (Car): Car park at Ground
Parking (Coach/Bus): Car park at Ground
Police Force and Tel No: Nottinghamshire (01623 420999)
Disabled Visitors' Facilities
  Wheelchairs: Bishop Street (Entrance at North end of West stand)
  Blind: Commentary available
Anticipated Development(s): There are long term plans for a move to a new stadium but, at this stage, there is no definite date.

KEY

C Club Offices
E Entrance(s) for visiting supporters

↑ North direction (approx)

❶ Car Park
❷ Quarry Lane
❸ A60 Nottingham Road to M1 Junction 27
❹ Portland Street
❺ To A38 and M1 Junction 28
❻ Town Centre

Left:
The familiar — and hirsute — figure of Brian Kilcline now plies his trade for Town. He is seen in action during the home 3rd Division clash with Cardiff City on 8 March 1997.

MIDDLESBROUGH

The Cellnet Riverside Stadium, Middlesbrough, Cleveland

Tel No: 01642 8777700
Ticket Office: 01642 877745
Fax: 01642 877840
League: 1st Division
Brief History: Founded 1876. Former Grounds: Archery Ground (Albert Park), Breckon Hill Road, Linthorpe Road, moved to Ayresome Park in 1903, and to current ground in Summer 1995. FA Amateur Cup winners 1894 and 1897 (joined Football League in 1899). Record attendance (Ayresome Park) 53,596, (Riverside Stadium) 30,215.
(Total) Current Capacity: Approx. 30,000 (all seated)
Visiting Supporters' Allocation: 3,470 (in the South Stand)

Club Colours: Red shirts, white shorts
Nearest Railway Station: Middlesbrough
Parking (Car): All parking at stadium is for permit holders.
Parking (Coach/Bus): As directed
Police Force and Tel No: Cleveland (01642 248184)
Disabled Visitors' Facilities
   Wheelchairs: More than 300 places available for disabled fans.
   Blind: Commentary available.
Anticipated Development(s): Plans are in hand for the construction of the missing two corner stands to increase capacity to c35,000.

KEY
C Club Offices
S Club Shop

↑ North direction (approx)

❶ Cargo Fleet Road
❷ To Middlesbrough station (0.5 miles)
❸ Middlesbrough town centre
❹ Middlesbrough Docks (1 mile) and Town Centre
❺ A66
❻ Station Street (leading to Borough Road)
❼ Car Park
❽ South Stand

Left:

It is doubtful whether any Middlesbrough supporters will forget the 1996/97 season. Docked three points by the FA for failing to fulfil the Premiership game at Blackburn, the team was destined to spend the entire season in an eventually unsuccessful battle against relegation; despite the atrocious league form, however, the team reached two cup finals — one via a replay with lowly Chesterfield — losing the Coca-Cola Cup to Leicester and the FA Cup to Chelsea, thereby achieving a unique treble in the history of English football (relegation and losing two cup finals in the space of one season — quite a record!!). Bryan Robson's expensively acquired team — including such stars as Italian Fabrizio Ravanelli illustrated here — was never consistent and often seemed to be wracked with internal dissension. It will be interesting to see how many of the team's expensive stars will still be around for trips to romantic points like Stockport and Bury.

MILLWALL

New Den, Bolina Road, London, SE16 3LN

Tel No: 0171 232 1222
Advance Tickets Tel No: 0171 231 9999
Fax: 0171 231 1662
League: 2nd Division
Brief History: Founded 1885 as Millwall Rovers, changed name to Millwall Athletic (1889) and Millwall (1925). Former Grounds: Glengall Road, East Ferry Road (2 separate Grounds), North Greenwich Ground and The Den - Cold Blow Lane - moved to New Den 1993/94 season. Founder-members Third Division (1920). Record attendance (at The Den) 48,672.

(Total) Current Capacity: 20,150 (20,150 seated)
Visiting Supporters' Allocation: 4,382
Club Colours: Royal Blue shirts, silver shorts
Nearest Railway Station: South Bermondsey Surrey Docks (tube)
Parking (Car): Juno Way car parking (8 mins. wal
Parking (Coach/Bus): At Ground
Police Force and Tel No: Metropolitan (0171 679 9217)
Disabled Visitors' Facilities
  Wheelchairs: Area allocated
  Blind: Commentary available

KEY
- **C** Club Offices
- **S** Club Shop
- **E** Entrance(s) for visiting supporters

↑ North direction (approx)

❶ Bolina Road
❷ South Bermondsey BR
❸ Surrey Quays Underground
❹ Zampa Road
❺ Ilderton Road
❻ To Rotherhithe New Road and Rotherhithe Tunnel
❼ To New Cross
❽ Surrey Canal Road

Left:

A disastrous season for the Lions saw the team fail to maintain a promotion push following relegation to the 2nd Division at the end of the 1995/96 season Matters were complicated by the club's worsening financial position. One high profile arrival during the season was ex-QPR boss Ray Wilkins — seen here with Tony Dolby during the Auto Windscreen match against Colchester on 7 January 1997 — who resumed a full time playing career with the team after a brief sojourn in Scotland.

NEWCASTLE UNITED

St. James' Park, Newcastle-upon-Tyne, NE1 4ST

Tel No: 0191 201 8400
Advance Tickets Tel No: 0191 261 1571
Fax: 0191 201 8600
League: F. A. Premier
Brief History: Founded in 1882 as Newcastle East End, changed to Newcastle United in 1892. Former Grounds: Chillingham Road, moved to St. James' Park (former home of defunct Newcastle West End) in 1892. Record attendance 68,386.
(Total) Current Capacity: 37,000 (all seated)
Visiting Supporters' Allocation: 1,862
Club Colours: Black & white striped shirts, black shorts
Nearest Railway Station: Newcastle Central

Parking (Car): Leazes car park & street parking
Parking (Coach/Bus): Leazes car park
Police Force and Tel No: Northumbria (0191 232 3451)
Disabled Visitors' Facilities
  Wheelchairs: Sir John Hall Stand
  Blind: Commentary available
Anticipated Development(s): Despite the expenditure in recent years at St James' Park, the club plans to move to a new 55,000 capacity ground in the Castle Leazes area of the city. There is local opposition to the choice of location, so nothing is as yet confirmed with regards to likely completion date.

KEY

C Club Offices
E Entrance(s) for visiting supporters
S Club Shop

⬆ North direction (approx)

❶ St. James' Street
❷ Strawberry Place
❸ Gallowgate
❹ Wellington Street
❺ To Newcastle Central BR Station (1/2 mile) & A6127 (M)
❻ Car Park
❼ Barrack Road (A189)
❽ To A1 and North
❾ Corporation Street
❿ Percy Street
⓫ Metro Station

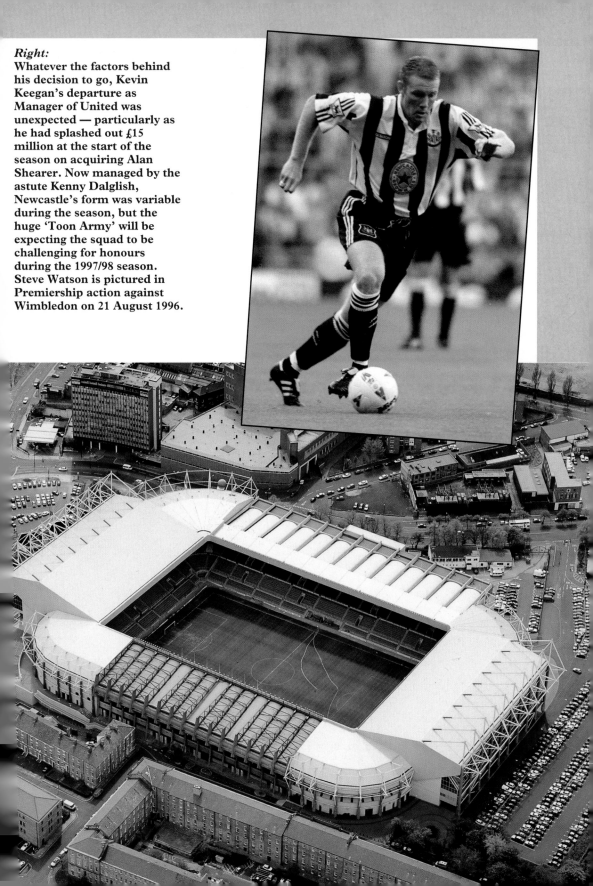

Right:
Whatever the factors behind his decision to go, Kevin Keegan's departure as Manager of United was unexpected — particularly as he had splashed out £15 million at the start of the season on acquiring Alan Shearer. Now managed by the astute Kenny Dalglish, Newcastle's form was variable during the season, but the huge 'Toon Army' will be expecting the squad to be challenging for honours during the 1997/98 season. Steve Watson is pictured in Premiership action against Wimbledon on 21 August 1996.

NORTHAMPTON TOWN

Sixfields Stadium, Northampton, NN5 5QA

Tel No: 01604 757773
Ticket Office: 01604 588338
Fax: 01604 751613
League: 2nd Division
Brief History: Founded 1897. Former, County, Ground was part of Northamptonshire County Cricket Ground. Moved to Sixfields Stadium during early 1994/95 season. Record attendance 24,523 (at County Ground)
(Total) Current Capacity: 7,653 (all seated)
Visiting Supporters' Allocation: 1,367 (all seated)

Club Colours: Claret shirts, White shorts
Nearest Railway Station: Northampton Castle
Parking (Car): Adjacent to Ground
Parking (Coach/Bus): Adjacent to Ground
Police Force and Tel No: Northants (01604 33221)
Disabled Visitors' Facilities
   Wheelchairs: Available on all four sides.
   Blind: Available.

KEY

C Club Offices
S Club Shop
E Entrance(s) for visiting supporters
R Refreshment bars for visiting supporters
T Toilets for visiting supporters

↑ North direction (approx)

❶ Weedon Road to Town Centre and Northampton Castle BR station (two miles)
❷ Upton Way, to M1 Junction 15A
❸ A45, to M1 Junction 16
❹ Car parks

ght:
he 1996/97 season was one
some success on the
ld for Northampton,
inging a Play-Off spot
d eventual victory over
vansea City at Wembley
24 May 1997, thereby
suring the Cobblers'
omotion in the team's
ntenary year. Town's
son White is caught
ring the first round FA
up match against
atford on 17 November
96.

NORWICH CITY

Carrow Road, Norwich, NR1 1JE

Tel No: 01603 760760
Advance Tickets Tel No: 01603 761661
Fax: 01603 613886
League: 1st Division
Brief History: Founded 1902. Former grounds: Newmarket Road and the Nest, Rosary Road; moved to Carrow Road in 1935. Founder members 3rd Division (1920). Record attendance 43,984.
(Total) Current Capacity: 21,994 (seated)

Visiting Supporters' Allocation: 1,741
Club Colours: Yellow shirts, yellow shorts
Nearest Railway Station: Norwich
Parking (Car): City centre car parks
Parking (Coach/Bus): Lower Clarence Road
Police Force and Tel No: Norfolk (01603 621212)
Disabled Visitors' Facilities
  Wheelchairs: South Stand (heated)
  Blind: No special facility

KEY

C   Club Offices
S   Club Shop
E   Entrance(s) for visiting supporters

↑   North direction (approx)

❶   Carrow Road
❷   A47 King Street
❸   River Wensum
❹   Riverside
❺   Car Park
❻   Norwich BR Station

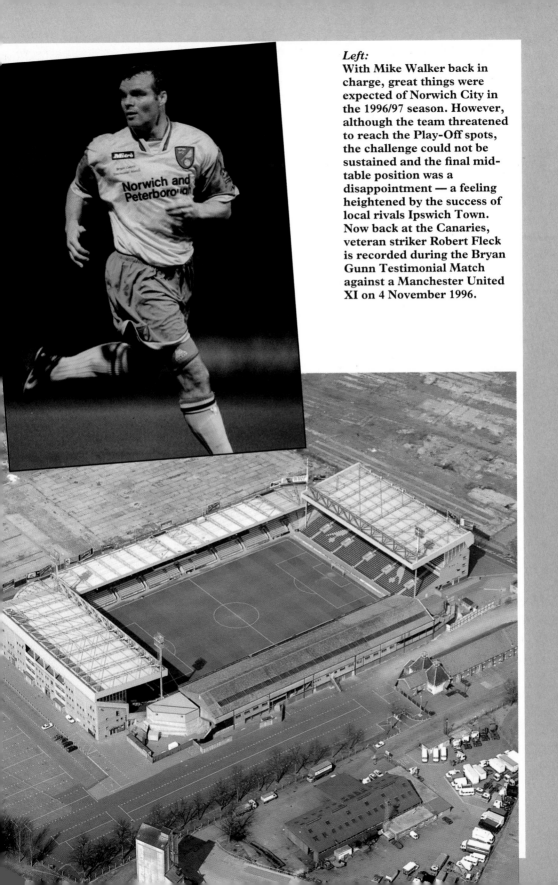

Left:

With Mike Walker back in charge, great things were expected of Norwich City in the 1996/97 season. However, although the team threatened to reach the Play-Off spots, the challenge could not be sustained and the final mid-table position was a disappointment — a feeling heightened by the success of local rivals Ipswich Town. Now back at the Canaries, veteran striker Robert Fleck is recorded during the Bryan Gunn Testimonial Match against a Manchester United XI on 4 November 1996.

NOTTINGHAM FOREST

City Ground, Nottingham, NG2 5FJ

Tel No: 0115 982 4444
Advance Tickets Tel No: 0115 982 4445
Fax: 0115 982 4456
League: 1st Division
Brief History: Founded 1865 as Forest Football Club, changed name to Nottingham Forest (c.1879). Former Grounds: Forest Recreation Ground, Meadow Cricket Ground, Trent Bridge (Cricket Ground), Parkside, Gregory Ground & Town Ground, moved to City Ground in 1898. Founder-members of Second Division (1892). Record attendance 49,945.

(Total) Current capacity: 30,602 (all seated)
Visiting Supporters' Allocation: Approx 5,1
Club Colours: Red shirts, white shorts
Nearest Railway Station: Nottingham Midlan
Parking (Car): East car park & street parking
Parking (Coach/Bus): East car park
Police Force and Tel No: Nottinghamshire (0115 948 1888)
Disabled Visitors' Facilities
  Wheelchairs: Front of Executive Stand
  Blind: No special facility

KEY

C Club Offices
S Club Shop
E Entrance(s) for visiting supporters

↑ North direction (approx)

❶ Radcliffe Road
❷ Lady Bay Bridge Road
❸ Trent Bridge
❹ Trent Bridge Cricket Ground
❺ Notts County F.C.
❻ River Trent
❼ Nottingham Midland BR Station (1/2 mile)

Left:
A disaster of a season for Forest saw Frank Clark resign, a much-delayed take-over and — at the end of a season of under-achievement — relegation. Following Clark's departure stalwart defender Stuart Pearce was made Player-Manager, with Dave Bassett later brought in to assist him. Although Pearce's determination can never be doubted, Forest's inability to win games was to cost them their position in the top flight. Fans will be expecting the team, as before, to bounce right back. The now departed Pearce is caught making a typically determined run in the league game against Middlesbrough on 24 August 1996.

NOTTS COUNTY

Meadow Lane, Nottingham, NG2 3HJ

Tel No: 0115 952 9000
Advance Tickets Tel No: 0115 955 7210
Fax: 0115 955 3994
League: 3rd Division
Brief History: Founded 1862 (oldest club in Football League) as Nottingham, changed to Notts County in c.1882. Former Grounds: Notts Cricket Ground (Beeston), Castle Cricket Ground, Trent Bridge Cricket Ground, moved to Meadow Lane in 1910. Founder-members Football League (1888). Record attendance 47,910.
(Total) Current Capacity: 20,300 (seated)

Visiting Supporters' Allocation: 5,438 (seat
Club Colours: Black & white striped shirts, bla
shorts.
Nearest Railway Station: Nottingham Midla
Parking (Car): Mainly street parking
Parking (Coach/Bus): Cattle market
Police Force and Tel No: Nottingham (0115
948 1888)
Disabled Visitors' Facilities
Wheelchairs: Meadow Lane/Jimmy Sirrel/Derek Pavis Stands.
Blind: No special facility

KEY

C Club Offices
S Club Shop
E Entrance(s) for visiting supporters
R Refreshment bars for visiting supporters
T Toilets for visiting supporters

↑ North direction (approx)

❶ A6011 Meadow Lane
❷ County Road
❸ A60 London Road
❹ River Trent
❺ Nottingham Midland BR Station (½ mile)

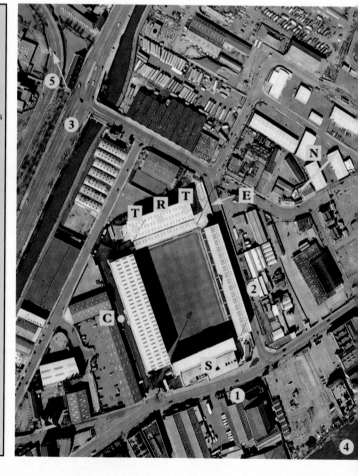

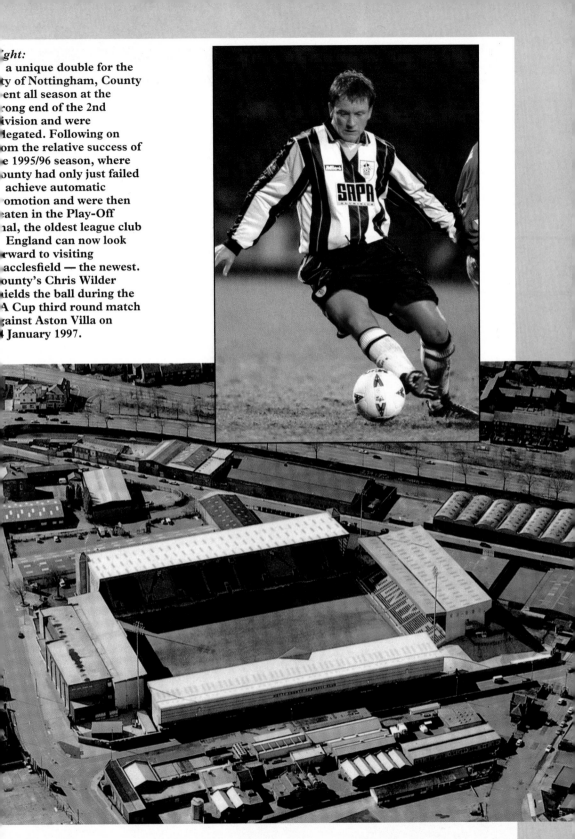

ght:

a unique double for the
ty of Nottingham, County
ent all season at the
rong end of the 2nd
ivision and were
legated. Following on
om the relative success of
e 1995/96 season, where
ounty had only just failed
achieve automatic
romotion and were then
eaten in the Play-Off
nal, the oldest league club
England can now look
rward to visiting
acclesfield — the newest.
ounty's Chris Wilder
ields the ball during the
A Cup third round match
ainst Aston Villa on
January 1997.

OLDHAM ATHLETIC

Boundary Park, Oldham, OL1 2PA

Tel No: 0161 624 4972
Advance Tickets Tel No: 0161 624 4972
Fax: 0161 652 6501
League: 2nd Division
Brief History: Founded 1897 as Pine Villa,
changed name to Oldham Athletic in 1899.
Former Grounds: Berry's Field, Pine Mill,
Athletic Ground (later named Boundary Park),
Hudson Fold, moved to Boundary Park in 1906.
Record attendance 47,671.
(Total) Current Capacity: 13,500 (all seated)
Visiting Supporters' Allocation: 1,800
minimum, 4,600 maximum

Club Colours: Blue and red shirts, white shor
Nearest Railway Station: Oldham Werneth
Parking (Car): Lookers Stand car park
Parking (Coach/Bus): At Ground
Police Force and Tel No: Greater Manchest
(0161 624 0444)
Disabled Visitors' Facilities
  Wheelchairs: Rochdale Road and Seton Sta
  Blind: No special facility
Anticipated Development(s): A new stand i
planned to replace the existing Lookers Stan
This will increase capacity at the ground to
some 23,000 when completed.

KEY

C Club Offices
E Entrance(s) for visiting
supporters

↑ North direction (approx)

❶ A663 Broadway
❷ Furtherwood Road
❸ Chadderton Way
❹ To A627(M) and M62
❺ To Oldham Werneth BR
Station (1¹/₂ miles)
❻ Car Park

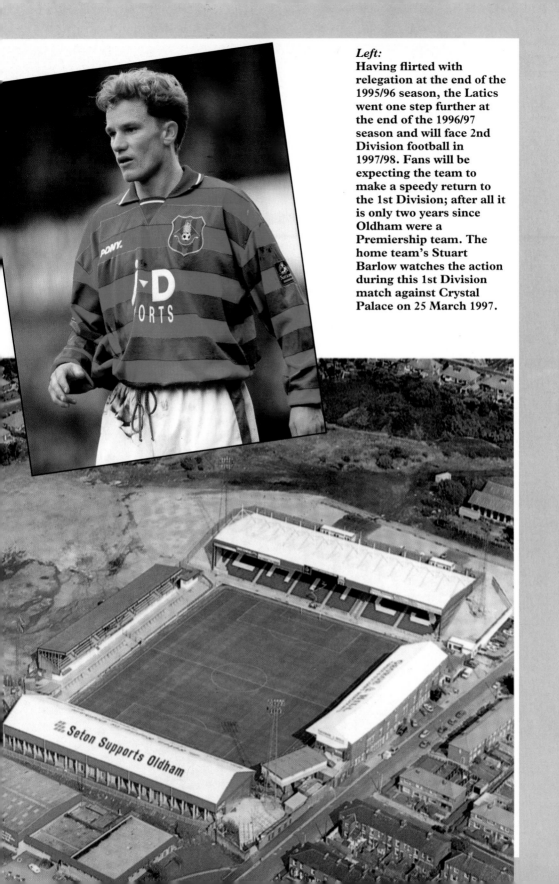

Left:
Having flirted with relegation at the end of the 1995/96 season, the Latics went one step further at the end of the 1996/97 season and will face 2nd Division football in 1997/98. Fans will be expecting the team to make a speedy return to the 1st Division; after all it is only two years since Oldham were a Premiership team. The home team's Stuart Barlow watches the action during this 1st Division match against Crystal Palace on 25 March 1997.

OXFORD UNITED

Manor Ground, London Road, Headington, Oxford, OX3 7RS

Tel No: 01865 61503*
Advance Tickets Tel No: 01865 61503*
Fax: 01865 741820*
* These are the numbers currently allocated to the
  original Manor Ground. It is unclear whether they
  will be transferred to the new ground.
League: 1st Division
Brief History: Founded 1893 as Headington (later
  Headington United), changed name to Oxford
  United in 1960. Former grounds: Britannia Inn
  Field, Headington Quarry, Wooten's Field,
  Manor Ground, the Paddocks and the Manor
  Ground (again) from 1925 to 1997. Record
  attendance at the Manor Ground 22,730.
(Total) Current Capacity: 15,000
Visiting Supporters' Allocation: 5,000 maximum
  (North Stand)
Club Colours: Yellow with navy blue trim shirts,
  navy blue with yellow trim shorts

Nearest Railway Station: Oxford or Didcot
Parking (Cars): 2,000 space car park at ground
Parking (Coach/Bus): As directed
Police Force and Tel No: Thames Valley (01865
  777501)
Disabled Visitors' Facilities:
  Wheelchairs: 80 places around the ground
  Blind: Commentary available
Anticipated Development(s): Although the club
  planned to move into its new 15,000-seater
  stadium at the start of the 1997/98 season, this is
  likely to prove impractical and the current
  intention is that the new ground will be occupied
  during the course of the season. The information
  given here relates to the new ground. For details
  the old Manor Ground, please turn to page 192

KEY

↑ North direction (approx)

❶ Blackbird Leys Road
❷ Oxford Eastern by-pass
  (A4142)
❸ To Headington and M40
❹ Junction with A4158 to
  central Oxford via the Iffley
  Road
❺ Junction with A4074 to
  Reading
❻ Oxford Southern by-pass
  leading to Western by-pass
  (A34)
❼ Littlemore
❽ Blackbird Leys estate
❾ A4077 Grenoble Road
❿ North Stand (away)
⓫ South Stand
⓬ Parking

ght:

season of consolidation
Oxford United in what
s supposed to be the
m's farewell year at the
anor Ground, saw
ited retain their 1st
vision status. One factor
the team's survival was
goal scoring form of
gel Jemson, seen here
ring the league
counter with Manchester
ty on 2 February 1997.
nson completed a
ccessful season by
abbing a couple of goals
Oxford's demolition of
omoted Barnsley in the
t game of the season.

PETERBOROUGH UNITED

London Road, Peterborough, Cambs, PE2 8AL

Tel No: 01733 63947
Advance Tickets Tel No: 01733 63947
Fax: 01733 557210
League: 3rd Division
Brief History: Founded in 1934, (no connection with former 'Peterborough and Fletton United' FC). Elected to Football League in 1960. Record attendance 30,096.
(Total) Current Capacity: 15,000 (9,800 seated)
Visiting Supporters' Allocation: 3,888 (888 seated)
Club Colours: Blue shirts, white shorts

Nearest Railway Station: Peterborough
Parking (Car): At ground
Parking (Coach/Bus): At ground
Police Force and Tel No: Cambridgeshire (01733 63232)
Disabled Visitors' Facilities
  Wheelchairs: Freemans Stand
  Blind: Commentary available
Future Development(s): The next phase in t[...] redevelopment of the ground, following the completion of the Freeman's Stand, will see [...] disappearance of the Moys End. The work h[...] as yet, no start date.

KEY

C Club Offices
S Club Shop
E Entrance(s) for visiting supporters
R Refreshment bars for visiting supporters
T Toilets for visiting supporters

↑ North direction (approx)

❶ A15 London Road
❷ Car Parks
❸ Peterborough BR Station (1 mile)
❹ Glebe Road
❺ A605
❻ To A1 (5 miles)

Right:
Although the season ended on a high note — winning 1-0 at promotion chasing Brentford — Posh were already doomed to 3rd Division football despite the involvement of Barry Fry. One of the few triumphs in a otherwise disappointing season was a 5-1 win over non-league Enfield in an FA Cup replay on 17 December 1996. Martin Carruthers celebrates scoring one of Peterborough's quartet of goals during that win.

PLYMOUTH ARGYLE

Home Park, Plymouth, PL2 3DQ

Tel No: 01752 562561
Advance Tickets Tel No: 01752 562561
Fax: 01752 606167
League: 2nd Division
Brief History: Founded 1886 as Argyle Athletic Club, changed name to Plymouth Argyle in 1903. Founder-members Third Division (1920). Record attendance 43,596
(Total) Current Capacity: 19,900 (8,800 seated)
Visiting Supporters' Allocation: 2,940 (300 seated)
Club Colours: Green & white striped shirts, black shorts

Nearest Railway Station: Plymouth
Parking (Car): Car park adjacent
Parking (Coach/Bus): Central car park
Police Force and Tel No: Devon & Cornwall (01752 701188)
Disabled Visitors' Facilities
  Wheelchairs: Devonport End
  Blind: Commentary available
Anticipated Development(s): Although the club still has plans to relocate to a new 23,000 capacity stadium, the timetable for its completion has slipped with 1999/2000 looking the earliest date for the new stadium to be available.

KEY

C Club Offices
S Club Shop
E Entrance(s) for visiting supporters
R Refreshment bars for visiting supporters
T Toilets for visiting supporters

⬆ North direction (approx)

❶ Outland Road
❷ Car Park
❸ Devonport Road
❹ Central Park
❺ Town Centre & Plymouth BR Station (³/₄ mile)

Left:
Following their triumph in
the 3rd Division Play-Off
final at Wembley in May
1996, much was expected
of an ambitious Argyle
team in 1996/97.
Unfortunately, however,
the reality was that the
team struggled to establish
itself at ther higher level
and only escaped
relegation by a whisker.
Chris Curran waits for the
ball during this 3rd
Division encounter at
Rochdale on 27 April 1996.

PORTSMOUTH

Fratton Park, 57 Frogmore Road, Portsmouth, Hants, PO4 8R.

Tel No: 01705 731204
Advance Tickets Tel No: 01705 618777
Fax: 01705 734129
League: 1st Division
Brief History: Founded 1898. Founder-members Third Division (1920). Record attendance 51,385.
(Total) Current Capacity: 20,000 (all seated) once North Stand completed
Visiting Supporters' Allocation: 3,020 (max) in Milton Stand
Club Colours: Blue shirts, white shorts
Nearest Railway Station: Fratton
Parking (Car): Street parking
Parking (Coach/Bus): As directed by Police

Police Force and Tel No: Hampshire (01705 321111)
Disabled Visitors' Facilities
  Wheelchairs: Frogmore Road
  Blind: No special facility
Anticipated Development(s): Tentative plan for a new ground at Parkway have been abandoned. The club now plans to take one of three options. One would involve the reconstruction of the existing Fratton Park; the second would see a realignment of the existing ground; and the third would see the club develop old railway land to the west of the old ground.

KEY
- **C** Club Offices
- **S** Club Shop
- **E** Entrance(s) for visiting supporters
- **R** Refreshment bars for visiting supporters
- **T** Toilets for visiting supporters

↑ North direction (approx)

❶ Alverstone Road
❷ Carisbrook Road
❸ A288 Milton Road
❹ A2030 Eastern Road to A27
❺ A2030 Goldsmith Avenue
❻ Fratton BR Station (½ mile)

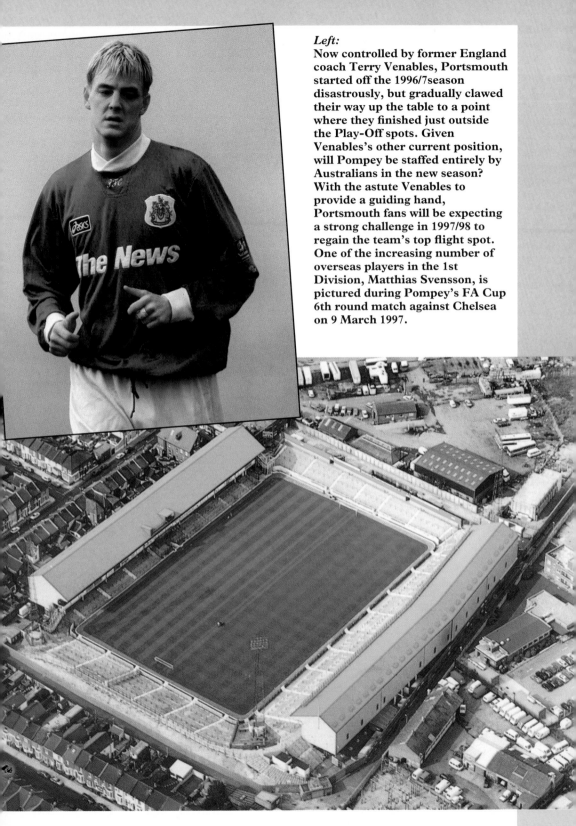

Left:
Now controlled by former England coach Terry Venables, Portsmouth started off the 1996/7season disastrously, but gradually clawed their way up the table to a point where they finished just outside the Play-Off spots. Given Venables's other current position, will Pompey be staffed entirely by Australians in the new season? With the astute Venables to provide a guiding hand, Portsmouth fans will be expecting a strong challenge in 1997/98 to regain the team's top flight spot. One of the increasing number of overseas players in the 1st Division, Matthias Svensson, is pictured during Pompey's FA Cup 6th round match against Chelsea on 9 March 1997.

PORT VALE

Vale Park, Burslem, Stoke-on-Trent, ST6 1AW

Tel No: 01782 814134
Advance Tickets Tel No: 01782 814134
Fax: 01782 834981
E-Mail: pvfc@port-vale.co.uk
League: 1st Division
Brief History: Founded 1876 as Burslem Port Vale, changed name to 'Port Vale' in 1907 (reformed club). Former Grounds: The Meadows Longport, Moorland Road Athletic Ground, Cobridge Athletic Grounds, Recreation Ground Hanley, moved to Vale Park in 1950. Founder-members Second Division (1892). Record attendance 50,000.

(Total) Current Capacity: 22,356 (17,616 seated)
Visiting Supporters' Allocation: 4,550
Club Colours: White shirts, black shorts
Nearest Railway Station: Longport (two mile
Parking (Car): Car park at Ground
Parking (Coach/Bus): Hamil Road car park
Police Force and Tel No: Staffordshire (0178 577114)
Disabled Visitors' Facilities
   Wheelchairs: Specialist Stand - Lorne Street
   Blind: Commentary available

KEY
C Club Offices
E Entrance(s) for visiting supporters

↑ North direction (approx)

❶ Car Parks
❷ Hamil Road
❸ Lorne Street
❹ B5051 Moorland Road

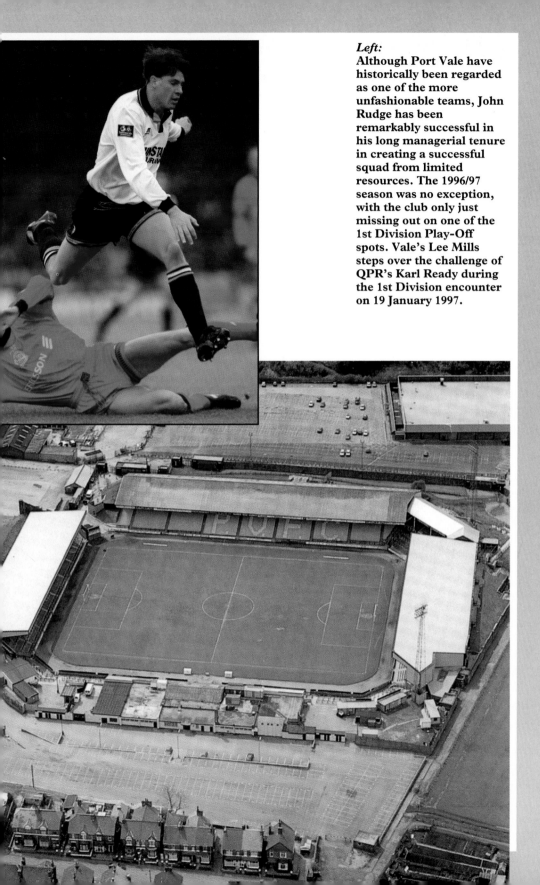

Left:
Although Port Vale have historically been regarded as one of the more unfashionable teams, John Rudge has been remarkably successful in his long managerial tenure in creating a successful squad from limited resources. The 1996/97 season was no exception, with the club only just missing out on one of the 1st Division Play-Off spots. Vale's Lee Mills steps over the challenge of QPR's Karl Ready during the 1st Division encounter on 19 January 1997.

PRESTON NORTH END

Lowthorpe Road, Deepdale, PR1 6RU

Tel No: 01772 902020
Advance Tickets Tel No: 01772 902000
Fax: 01772 653266
League: 2nd Division
Brief History: Founded 1867 as a Rugby Club, changed to soccer in 1881. Former ground: Moor park, moved to (later named) Deepdale in 1875. Founder-members Football League (1888). Record attendance 42,684.
(Total) Current Capacity: 15,295 (9,131 seated)
Visiting Supporters' Allocation: 2,667 maximum
Club Colours: White shirts, blue shorts

Nearest Railway Station: Preston (2 miles)
Parking (Car): West Stand car park
Parking (Coach/Bus): West Stand car park
Police Force and Tel No: Lancashire (01772 203203)
Disabled Visitors' Facilities
  Wheelchairs: Tom Finney Stand
  Blind: Earphones Commentary
Anticipated Development(s): With the completion of the dramatic Tom Finney stand (face *et al*), the next phase in the ground's redevelopment is likely to affect the Fulwood End.

KEY
C Club Offices
S Club Shop

↑ North direction (approx)

❶ A6033 Deepdale Road
❷ Lawthorpe Road
❸ Car Park
❹ A5085 Blackpool Road
❺ Preston BR Station (2 miles)
❻ Fulwood End – Spion Kop
❼ Tom Finney Stand

Left:
North End's first season back in the 2nd Division was a struggle, but a mid-table position at the end of the year will no doubt lead to higher expectations in 1997/98. Mike Flynn and Gary Swann battle with Stockport County's striker Kevin Francis during the league encounter on 18 February 1997.

QUEENS PARK RANGERS

Rangers Stadium, South Africa Road, London, W12 7PA

Tel No: 0181 743 0262
Tickets and Info. Tel No: 0181 740 0610
Fax: 0181 749 0994
League: 1st Division
Brief History: Founded 1885 as 'St. Jude's Institute', amalgamated with Christchurch Rangers to become Queens Park Rangers in 1886. Football League record number of former Grounds and Ground moves (13 different venues, 17 changes), including White City Stadium (twice) final move to Rangers Stadium (then named Loftus Road) in 1963. Founder-members Third Division (1920). Record attendance 35,353.
(Total) Current Capacity: 19,074 (all seated)

Visiting Supporters' Allocation: 3,100
Club Colours: Blue & white hooped shirts, whi shorts
Nearest Railway Station: Shepherds Bush and White City (both tube)
Parking (Car): White City NCP & street parking
Parking (Coach/Bus): White City NCP
Police Force and Tel No: Metropolitan (0181 246 2725)
Disabled Visitors' Facilities
  Wheelchairs: Ellerslie Road Stand & West Paddock
  Blind: Ellerslie Road Stand

KEY

C Club Offices
S Club Shop
E Entrance(s) for visiting supporters

↑ North direction (approx)

❶ South Africa Road
❷ To White City Tube Station, A219 Wood Lane and A40 Western Avenue
❸ A4020 Uxbridge Road
❹ To Shepherds Bush Tube Station
❺ Ellerslie Road
❻ BBC Television Centre
❼ Loftus Road
❽ Bloemfontein Road

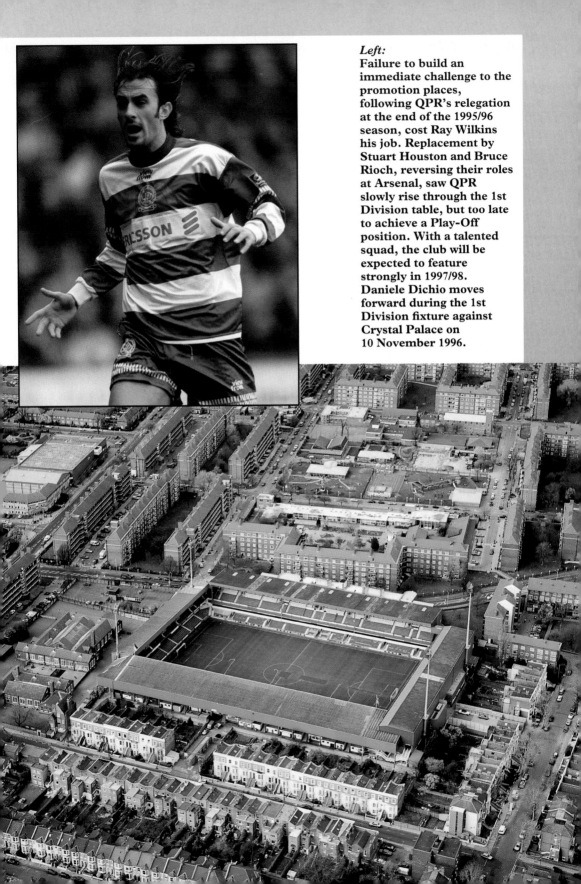

Left:
Failure to build an
immediate challenge to the
promotion places,
following QPR's relegation
at the end of the 1995/96
season, cost Ray Wilkins
his job. Replacement by
Stuart Houston and Bruce
Rioch, reversing their roles
at Arsenal, saw QPR
slowly rise through the 1st
Division table, but too late
to achieve a Play-Off
position. With a talented
squad, the club will be
expected to feature
strongly in 1997/98.
Daniele Dichio moves
forward during the 1st
Division fixture against
Crystal Palace on
10 November 1996.

READING

Elm Park, Norfolk Road, Reading, RG3 2EF

Tel No: 0118 950 7878
Advance Tickets Tel No: 0118 950 7878
Fax: 0118 956 6682
League: 1st Division
Brief History: Founded 1871. (Amalgamated with Reading Hornets in 1877 and with Earley in 1889.) Former Grounds: Reading Recreation Ground, Reading Cricket Ground, Coley Park and Caversham Cricket Ground, moved to Elm Park in 1895. Founder-members Third Division (1920). Record attendance 33,042.
(Total) Current Capacity: 15,000 (2,242 seated)
Visiting Supporters' Allocation: 3,114 (282 seated)
Club Colours: White with blue hoops shirts, white shorts

Nearest Railway Station: Reading West
Parking (Car): Street parking & Park & Ride scheme from Prospect School, Honey End Lane.
Parking (Coach/Bus): The Meadway
Police Force and Tel No: Thames Valley (011 953 6000)
Disabled Visitors' Facilities
  Wheelchairs: Norfolk Road
  Blind: Organised by Hospital Radio
Anticipated Development(s): Initial plans to relocate to a new ground at the start of 1997/ proved optimistic. Work will, however, start o a new 25,000 all-seater stadium at Smallmead to enable the club to occupy it from the start the 1998/99 season.

KEY

C Club Offices
S Club Shop
E Entrance(s) for visiting supporters
R Refreshment bars for visiting supporters
T Toilets for visiting supporters

↑ North direction (approx)

❶ Tilehurst Road
❷ Norfolk Road
❸ County Cricket Ground
❹ Reading West BR Station (½ mile)
❺ Liebenrood Road to A4 Bath Road (¼ mile)

Left:
Another season of limited
success saw Reading
marooned in the lower half of
the 1st Division; never quite
getting sucked into the
relegation mire, the team also
never threatened to repeat its
near promotion of two years
ago. Mick Gooding, one of the
club's then co-managers (who
were dismissed at the end of
the season), competes for the
ball in the league encounter
against Wolves on 5 October
1996.

ROCHDALE

Willbutts Lane, Spotland, Rochdale, OL11 5DS

Tel No: 01706 44648
Advance Tickets Tel No: 01706 44648
Fax: 01706 48466
League: 3rd Division
Brief History: Founded 1907 from former Rochdale Town F.C. (founded 1900). Founder-members Third Division North (1921). Record attendance 24,231.
(Total) Current Capacity: 9,032 (4,638 seated) following completion of Pearl Street Stand
Visiting Supporters' Allocation: 2,750 (250 seated)
Club Colours: Blue shirts, white shorts

Nearest Railway Station: Rochdale
Parking (Car): Rear of ground
Parking (Coach/Bus): Rear of ground
Police Force and Tel No: Greater Manchester (01706 47401)
Disabled Visitors' Facilities
  Wheelchairs: Main stand - disabled area
  Blind: Commentary available
Anticipated Development(s): With the forthcoming completion of the new Pearl Street Stand, attention will turn to the Willbutts Lane Terrace, although there is as yet no definite start date.

KEY

C Club Offices
S Club Shop
E Entrance(s) for visiting supporters
R Refreshment bars for visiting supporters
T Toilets for visiting supporters

↑ North direction (approx)

❶ Willbutts Lane
❷ A627 Edenfield Road
❸ Rochdale BR Station (1/2 mile)
❹ Sandy Lane
❺ To M62
❻ To M65 and North
❼ Pearl Street Stand (under construction)

Left:
A disappointing season for the team saw Rochdale achieve no more than a mid-table position in the 3rd Division. Unless things dramatically improve it is unlikely that the 9,000 capacity of Spotland following completion of the new Pearl Street Stand will be needed on a regular basis. Dave Thanpson keeps a careful eye on the ball during this 3rd Division encounter with Plymouth on 27 April 1996.

ROTHERHAM UNITED

Millmoor Ground, Rotherham, S60 1HR

Tel No: 01709 512434
Advance Tickets Tel No: 01709 512434
Fax: 01709 512762
League: 3rd Division
Brief History: Founded 1877 (as Thornhill, later Thornhill United), changed name to Rotherham County in 1905 and to Rotherham United in 1925, (amalgamated with Rotherham Town - Football League members 1893-97 - in 1925). Former Grounds include: Red House Ground & Clifton Lane Cricket Ground, moved to Millmoor in 1907. Record attendance 25,000.
(Total) Current Capacity: 11,489 (4,442 seated)

Visiting Supporters' Allocation: 4,219 (1,094 seated)
Club Colours: Red shirts, white shorts
Nearest Railway Station: Rotherham Central
Parking (Car): Kimberworth and Main Street car parks, plus large car park adjacent to ground.
Parking (Coach/Bus): As directed by Police
Police Force and Tel No: South Yorkshire (01709 371121)
Disabled Visitors' Facilities
  Wheelchairs: Millmoor Lane
  Blind: Commentary available

KEY

C Club Offices
S Club Shop
E Entrance(s) for visiting supporters
R Refreshment bars for visiting supporters
T Toilets for visiting supporters

↑ North direction (approx)

❶ Car Park
❷ Rotherham Central BR Station
❸ A6109 Masborough Road
❹ Millmoor Lane
❺ To A6178 and M1 Junction 34

Left:
The 1995/96 season ended in triumph with the club's first ever triumph at Wembley in the Auto Windscreen trophy over Shrewsbury Town; at the end of the 1996/97 season both clubs shared another (less successful) attribute — relegation to the 3rd Division. Struggling throughout the season, only Notts County kept United off the bottom. United's Eary Bowter competes for the ball with Bristol City's Martin Kuhl during this 2nd Division encounter towards the end of the 1995/96 season.

SCARBOROUGH

McCain Stadium, Seamer Road, Scarborough, N. Yorkshire YO12 4HI

Tel No: 01723 375094

Advance Tickets Tel No: 01723 375094

Fax: 01723 378733

League: 3rd Division

Brief History: Founded 1879 as 'Scarborough Cricketers F.C.' changed name to 'Scarborough F.C.' in 1887. Former grounds: North Marine (Cricket) Ground and Recreation Ground, moved to (then named) Athletic Ground in 1898. Promoted to Football League in 1987. Record attendance 11,124.

(Total) Current Capacity: 6,230 (3,379 seated)

Visiting Supporters' Allocation: 1,336 (all seated)

Club Colours: Red shirts, white shorts

Nearest Railway Station: Scarborough Centra (2 miles)

Parking (Car): Street parking

Parking (Coach/Bus): Weaponess coach/car park

Police Force and Tel No: North Yorkshire (01723 500300)

Disabled Visitors' Facilities

Wheelchairs: Main Stand, Edgehill Road end

Blind: No special facility

Anticipated Development(s): The next area of the ground to receive attention is McCain stand, which will see the roof extended over both corners. A definite start date has yet to be confirmed, but it could be during the 1997/98 season.

KEY
C Club Offices
S Club Shop
E Entrance(s) for visiting supporters
R Refreshment bars for visiting supporters
T Toilets for visiting supporters

⬆ North direction (approx)

❶ A64 Seamer Road
❷ Scarborough Central BR Station (2 miles)
❸ To York
❹ McCain Stand
❺ Hinderwell Road
❻ Edgehill Road
❼ Seamer Road Stand
❽ Edgehill Road Stand

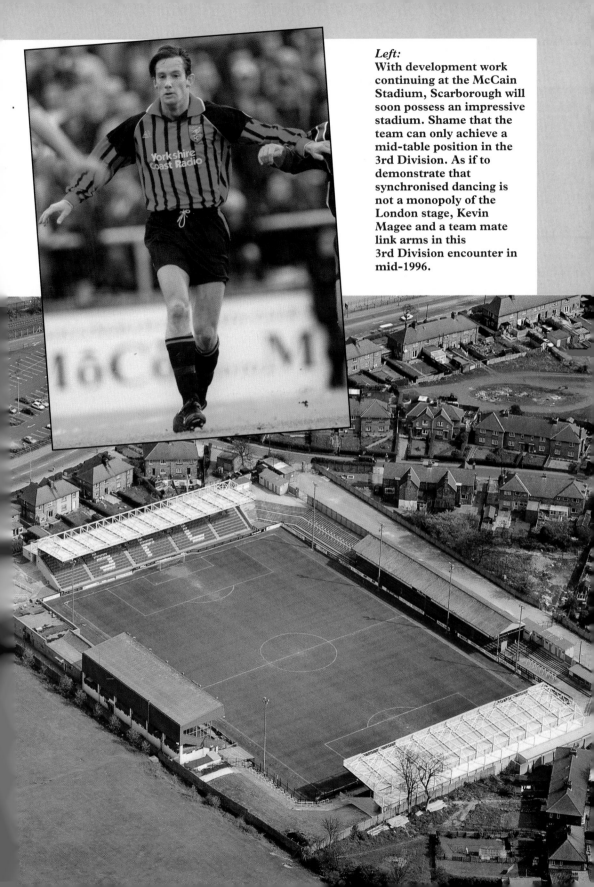

Left:
With development work continuing at the McCain Stadium, Scarborough will soon possess an impressive stadium. Shame that the team can only achieve a mid-table position in the 3rd Division. As if to demonstrate that synchronised dancing is not a monopoly of the London stage, Kevin Magee and a team mate link arms in this 3rd Division encounter in mid-1996.

SCUNTHORPE UNITED

Glanford Park, Doncaster Road, Scunthorpe DN15 8TD

Tel No: 01724 848077
Advance Tickets Tel No: 01724 848077
Fax: 01724 857986
League: 3rd Division
Brief History: Founded 1899 as Scunthorpe United, amalgamated with North Lindsey to become 'Scunthorpe & Lindsey United in 1912. Changed name to Scunthorpe United in 1956. Former grounds: Crosby (Lindsey United) & Old Showground, moved to Glanford Park in 1988. Elected to Football League in 1950. Record attendance 8,775 (23,935 at Old Showground).

(Total) Current Capacity: 9,200 (6,400 seated)
Visiting Supporters' Allocation: 1,678
Club Colours: Claret and blue shirts, blue shorts.
Nearest Railway Station: Scunthorpe
Parking (Car): At ground
Parking (Coach/Bus): At ground
Police Force and Tel No: Humberside (01724 282888)

Disabled Visitors' Facilities
 Wheelchairs: Clugston Stand
 Blind: Commentary available

KEY

C Club Offices
S Club Shop
E Entrance(s) for visiting supporters
R Refreshment bars for visiting supporters
T Toilets for visiting supporters

↑ North direction (approx)

❶ Car Park
❷ Glanford Stand
❸ A18 Scunthorpe BR Station and Town Centre (1½ miles)
❹ M181 and M180 Junction 3

Left:
Another mid-table position for Scunthorpe means that fans of Brian Laws' team will have the excuse of adding Macclesfield to their away days. Irons' David D'Auria is pictured in action in early 1996.

SHEFFIELD UNITED

Bramall Lane, Sheffield, S2 4SU

Tel No: 0114 221 5757
Advance Tickets Tel No: 0114 221 1889
Fax: 0114 272 3030
League: 1st Division
Brief History: Founded 1889. (Sheffield Wednesday occasionally used Bramall Lane c.1880). Founder-members 2nd Division (1892). Record attendance 68,287
(Total) Current Capacity: 30,370 (all seated)
Visiting Supporters' Allocation: 2,696 (seated)
Club Colours: Red & white striped shirts, black shorts

Nearest Railway Station: Sheffield Midland
Parking (Car): Street parking
Parking (Coach/Bus): As directed by Police
Police Force and Tel No: South Yorkshire (0114 276 8522)
Disabled Visitors' Facilities
  Wheelchairs: John Street South Stand
  Blind: Commentary available
Anticipated Development(s): None planned following the completion of the John Street Stand.

KEY

C Club Offices
S Club Shop
E Entrance(s) for visiting supporters

↑ North direction (approx)

❶ A621 Bramall Lane
❷ Shoreham Street
❸ Car Park
❹ Sheffield Midland BR Station (¼ mile)
❺ John Street
❻ Spion Kop
❼ John Street Stand

Left:
Finishing fifth in the 1st Division assured the Blades of a Play-Off semi-final against Ipswich Town. Victory by the away goals rule took United to the Play-Off Final, where the team lost to Crystal Palace. On 14 December 1996, Oxford United's Martin Aldridge gets sandwiched between Sheffield United's Lee Sandford and Roger Nilson in the league game at Oxford; if all goes to plan, this could have been the Blades' last visit to the Manor Ground.

SHEFFIELD WEDNESDAY

Hillsborough, Sheffield, S6 1SW

Tel No: 0114 221 2121
Advance Tickets Tel No: 0114 221 2400
Fax: 0114 221 2122
League: F.A. Premier
Brief History: Founded 1867 as The Wednesday F.C. (changed to Sheffield Wednesday c.1930). Former Grounds: London Road, Wyrtle Road (Heeley), Sheaf House Ground, Encliffe & Olive Grove (Bramall Lane also used occasionally), moved to Hillsborough (then named 'Owlerton' in 1899). Founder-members Second Division (1892). Record attendance 72,841.

(Total) Current Capacity: 39,814 (all seated)
Visiting Supporters' Allocation: 3,900 (all seated)
Club Colours: Blue & white striped shirts, blue shorts
Nearest Railway Station: Sheffield (4 miles)
Parking (Car): Street Parking
Parking (Coach/Bus): Owlerton Stadium
Police Force and Tel No: South Yorkshire (0114 234 3131)
Disabled Visitors' Facilities
    Wheelchairs: North and Lower West Stands
    Blind: Commentary available

KEY
C Club Offices
S Club Shop
E Entrance(s) for visiting supporters

↑ North direction (approx)

❶ Leppings Lane
❷ River Dom
❸ A61 Penistone Road North
❹ Sheffield BR Station and City Centre (4 miles)
❺ Spion Kop
❻ To M1 (North)
❼ To M1 (South)

148

Left:
A roller coaster of a season for Sheffield Wednesday saw David Pleat's team lead the table at the start of the season, then fall away before mounting a late (and unsuccessful) challenge for a European place. One of a number of foreign players in the team, Regi Blinker, dreadlocks flowing, strides purposefully forward in the Premiership fixture against Chelsea on 7 September 1996.

149

SHREWSBURY TOWN

Gay Meadow, Shrewsbury, SY2 6AB

Tel No: 01743 360111
Advance Tickets Tel No: 01743 360111
Fax: 01743 236384
League: 3rd Division
Brief History: Founded 1886. Former Grounds: Monkmoor Racecourse, Ambler's Field & The Barracks Ground (moved to Gay Meadow in 1910). Elected to Football League in 1950. Record attendance 18,917
(Total) Current Capacity: 7,500 (2,000 seated)
Visiting Supporters' Allocation: 2,500 (500 seated)
Club Colours: Blue with White shoulder shirts, blue shorts.

Nearest Railway Station: Shrewsbury
Parking (Car): Adjacent car park
Parking (Coach/Bus): Gay Meadow
Police Force and Tel No: West Mercia (01743 232888)
Disabled Visitors' Facilities
  Wheelchairs: Alongside Pitch (as directed)
  Blind: No special facility
Anticipated Development(s): If vague talk of relocation comes to nothing, then the club will redevelop Gay Meadow.

KEY
C Club Offices
S Club Shop
E Entrance(s) for visiting supporters
R Refreshment bars for visiting supporters
T Toilets for visiting supporters

↑ North direction (approx)

❶ Entrance road to ground
❷ Abbey Foregate
❸ River Severn
❹ Car Parks
❺ Shrewsbury BR Station (1 mile — shortest route)
❻ Riverside Terrace

Although the 1996/97 season started reasonably well for Town, as it progressed the team slowly sank down the 2nd Division table and, having lost to Wycombe Wanderers, was sucked into the mire at the foot of the table. Unable to escape the drop, Shrewsbury Town will be playing 3rd Division football in 1997/98 — a far cry from the club's first visit to Wembley at the end of 1996/97. Looking somewhat pensive — perhaps he had a foreboding about the season — Town's Mark Taylor is recorded in the home game against fellow strugglers Wycombe Wanderers on 18 August 1996.

SOUTHAMPTON

The Dell, Milton Road, Southampton, SO15 2XH

Tel No: 01703 220505
Advance Tickets Tel No: 01703 228575
Fax: 01703 330360
E-Mail: sfc@tcp.co.uk
League: F.A. Premier
Brief History: Founded 1885 as 'Southampton St. Mary's Young Mens Association' (changed name to Southampton in 1897). Former Grounds: Northlands Road, Antelope Ground, County Ground, moved to The Dell in 1898. Founder-members Third Division (1920). Record attendance 31,044.

(Total) Current Capacity: 15,250 (all seated)
Visiting Supporters' Allocation: 1,500 (all seated)
Club Colours: Red & white shirts, black shorts
Nearest Railway Station: Southampton
Parking (Car): Street parking
Parking (Coach/Bus): As directed by Police
Police Force and Tel No: Hampshire (01703 581111)
Disabled Visitors' Facilities
    Wheelchairs: Milton Road (book in advance)
    Blind: Commentary available (book in advance)

KEY

C Club Offices
S Club Shop
E Entrance(s) for visiting supporters
R Refreshment bars for visiting supporters
T Toilets for visiting supporters

↑ North direction (approx)

❶ Archers Road
❷ Milton Road
❸ Hill Lane
❹ To Southampton BR station
❺ To A33, M3 and the north

Right:
Another season, another manager, but still the struggle against relegation. Many pundits' favourites for the drop, Southampton under Graeme Souness seemed likely to fulfil the prophecies until an end of season rally brought the Saints another season in the top flight, although both Souness and Lawrie McMenemy resigned after the season's end. Dave Beasant practices his bowling action for the forthcoming cricket season during this Premiership match against eventual champions Manchester United on 26 October 1996.

SOUTHEND UNITED

Roots Hall Ground, Victoria Avenue, Southend-on-Sea, SS2 6N(

Tel No: 01702 304050
Advance Tickets Tel No: 01702 304090
Fax: 01702 330164
League: 2nd Division
Brief History: Founded 1906. Former
Grounds: Roots Hall, Kursaal, The Stadium
Grainger Road, moved to Roots Hall (new
Ground) 1955. Founder-members Third
Division (1920). Record attendance 31,033.
(Total) Current Capacity: 12,306 (all seated)

Visiting Supporters' Allocation: 3,974
Club Colours: Blue shirts, blue shorts
Nearest Railway Station: Prittlewell
Parking (Car): Street parking
Parking (Coach/Bus): Car park at Ground
Police Force and Tel No: Essex (01702 43121:
Disabled Visitors' Facilities
  Wheelchairs: West Stand
  Blind: Commentary available

KEY

C Club Offices

E Entrance(s) for visiting
supporters

R Refreshment bars for visiting
supporters

T Toilets for visiting supporters

⬆ North direction (approx)

❶ Director's Car Park
❷ Prittlewell BR Station
(¹/₄ mile)
❸ A127 Victoria Avenue
❹ Fairfax Drive
❺ Southend centre (¹/₂ mile)
❻ North Bank

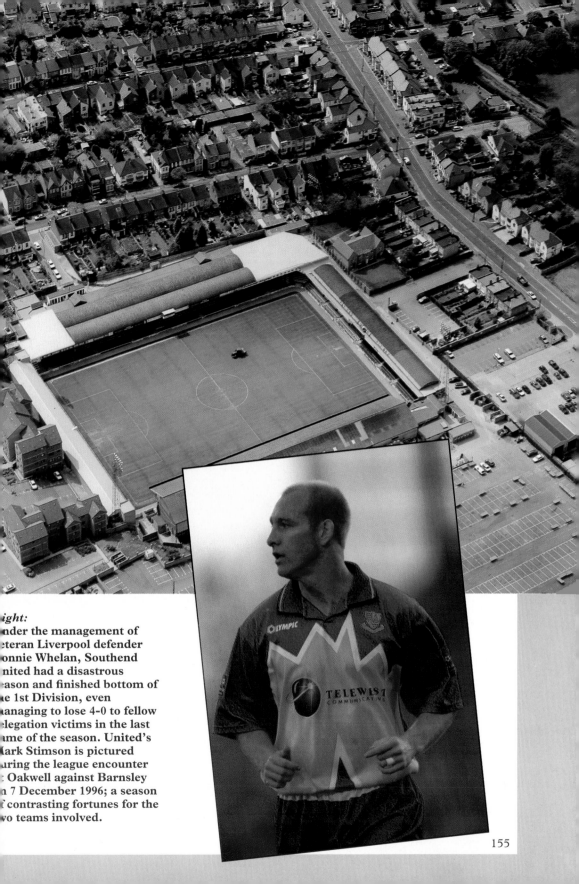

Right:
Under the management of veteran Liverpool defender Ronnie Whelan, Southend United had a disastrous season and finished bottom of the 1st Division, even managing to lose 4-0 to fellow relegation victims in the last game of the season. United's Mark Stimson is pictured during the league encounter at Oakwell against Barnsley on 7 December 1996; a season of contrasting fortunes for the two teams involved.

155

STOCKPORT COUNTY

Edgeley Park, Hardcastle Road, Edgeley, Stockport, SK3 9DD

Tel No: 0161 286 8888
Advance Tickets Tel No: 0161 286 8888
Fax: 0161 286 8900
League: 1st Division
Brief History: Founded 1883 as Heaton Norris
  Rovers, changed name to Stockport County in
  1890. Former Grounds: Heaton Norris
  Recreation Ground, Heaton Norris Wanderers
  Cricket Ground, Chorlton's Farm, Ash Inn
  Ground, Wilkes Field (Belmont Street) and
  Nursery Inn (Green Lane), moved to Edgeley
  Park in 1902. Record attendance 27,833.
(Total) Current Capacity: 12,160 (9,410
  seated)
Visiting Supporters' Allocation: 3,400

Club Colours: Blue shirts with red & white
  flashes, white shorts
Nearest Railway Station: Stockport
Parking (Car): Street parking
Parking (Coach/Bus): As directed by Police
Police Force and Tel No: Greater Manchester
  (0161 872 5050)
Disabled Visitors' Facilities
  Wheelchairs: Main Stand
  Blind: Headsets available
Anticipated Development(s): The next stage
  the ground's redevelopment will affect the
  Railway End. If work starts during the season,
  away fans will be relocated (probably to part o
  the Vernons Stand).

KEY

C Club Offices
E Entrance(s) for visiting
  supporters

↑ North direction (approx)

❶ Mercian Way
❷ Hardcastle Road
❸ Stockport BR Station
  (¼ mile)
❹ Railway End
❺ Main Stand
❻ Cheadle Stand

Left:
A great season for County saw the team promoted from the 2nd Division and reach the Coca-Cola Cup semi-final, where they lost eventually to Middlesbrough. Boro's Nigel Pearson out jumps County's Andy Mutch during the game at the Riverside Stadium on 12 March 1997. Ironically, it was a season of contrasts for the two teams; competition between the two will be resumed in the 1st Division in 1997/98.

STOKE CITY

Britannia Stadium, Stanley Matthews Way, Stoke-on-Trent

Tel No: 01782 413511*
Advance Tickets Tel No: 01782 413961*
Fax: 01782 745340*
  * Note: Telephone numbers are those of the Victoria Ground. At the time of writing it is uncertain whether these will be transferred to the new stadium.
League: 1st Division
Brief History: Founded 1863 as Stoke F.C., amalgamated with Stoke Victoria in 1878, changed to Stoke City in 1925. Former grounds: Sweetings Field, Victoria Ground (1878-1997), moved to new ground for start of 1997/98 season. Record attendance (at Victoria Ground): 51,380.
(Total) Current Capacity: 28,000 (all-seater)
Visiting Supporters' Allocation: 5,000 (in the South Stand)

Club Colours: Red & white striped shirts, white shorts
Nearest Railway Station: Stoke on Trent
Parking (Cars): 650 places at the ground plus 1,600 to the south of the ground. These will be for season ticket holders mainly. On-street parking in the grounds vicinity priced at £3.00
Parking (Coach/Bus): As directed
Police Force and Tel No: Staffordshire (01782 744644)
Disabled Visitors' Facilities:
  Wheelchairs: 164 places for disabled spectators
  Blind: No special facility
Anticipated Development(s): None following the completion of the new ground.

KEY

↑ North direction (approx)

❶ Victoria Ground
❷ Stoke BR station
❸ A500 Queensway
❹ North Stand
❺ West Stand
❻ East Stand
❼ South Stand (away)
❽ A50 to Uttoxeter
❾ To M6 northbound
❿ To M6 southbound

SUNDERLAND

Stadium of Light, Sunderland, SR5 1BT

Tel No: 0191 551 5000
Advance Tickets Tel No: 0191 551 5151
Fax: 0191 551 1234
League: 1st Division
Brief History: Founded 1879 as 'Sunderland & District Teachers Association', changed to 'Sunderland Association' in 1880 and shortly after to 'Sunderland'. Former Grounds: Blue House Field, Groves Field (Ashbrooke), Horatio Street, Abbs Field, Newcastle Road and Roker Park (1898-1997; moved to Stadium Park for the start of the 1997/98 season. Record crowd (at Roker Park): 75,118.
(Total) Current Capacity: 42,000 all-seater
Visiting Supporters' Allocation: 3,000 (South Stand)
Club Colours: red and white striped shirts, black shorts

Nearest Railway Station: Sunderland (one mile)
Parking (Cars): car park at ground reserved for season ticket holders. Limited on-street parking (but the police may decide to introduce restrictions). Otherwise off-street car parks in city centre.
Parking (Coach/Bus): As directed
Police Force and Tel No: Tyne & Wear (0191 567 6155)
Disabled Visitors' Facilities:
Wheelchairs: 300 spots
Blind: Commentary available
Anticipated Development(s): Although the ground is brand-new, there are plans to raise the capacity to 61,000 if needed.

KEY

⬆ North direction (approx)

❶ Roker Park
❷ North Stand
❸ South (Metro FM) Stand (away)
❹ To Sunderland BR station (0.5 mile)
❺ Southwick Road
❻ Wreath Quay Road
❼ Black Road
❽ Hay Street
❾ A1018 Newcastle Road
❿ To north (South Shields and Gateshead
⓫ A1018 North Bridge Street to Wearmouth Bridge and City Centre

Note: The names of Black Road and Wreath Quay Road are due to change.

Left:
Another club bidding farewell to its traditional home is Sunderland, who played their last game at Roker Park on 4 May 1997 before moving to the new ground at Monkwearmouth. Peter Reid's side initially performed well in the Premiership, before a mid-season decline led them into the struggle against relegation. Results later in the season, despite a win at fellow strugglers Middlesborough, were not enough to ensure that Sunderland's new stadium would be graced with Premiership football. One factor in Sunderland's late return to form was the arrival of Chris Waddle. Released by Sheffield Wednesday and rescued from relative obscurity at Falkirk by 1st Division strugglers Bradford City, Waddle's move back to his native northeast was not without its controversial moments. His first game against Nottingham Forest — pictured here on 22 March 1997 — was ironic, given that Forest themselves thought they had signed the veteran player.

161

SWANSEA CITY

Vetch Field, Swansea, SA1 3SU

Tel No: 01792 474114
Advance Tickets Tel No: 01792 474114
Fax: 01792 464120
League: 3rd Division
Brief History: Founded 1900 as Swansea Town, changed to Swansea City in 1970. Former Grounds: various, including Recreation Ground. Moved to Vetch Field in 1912. Founder-members Third Division (1920). Record attendance 32,796.
(Total) Current Capacity: 11,147 (3,635 seated)
Visiting Supporters' Allocation: 3,500

Club Colours: White shirts, white shorts
Nearest Railway Station: Swansea High Stree
Parking (Car): Kingsway car park & adjacent Clarence Terrace, (supervised car park).
Parking (Coach/Bus): As directed by Police
Police Force and Tel No: South Wales (0179 456999)
Disabled Visitors' Facilities
　Wheelchairs: Glamorgan Street
　Blind: No special facility
Anticipated Development(s): There are tentative plans for relocation, but nothing has been confirmed.

KEY

C Club Offices
S Club Shop
E Entrance(s) for visiting supporters

↑ North direction (approx)

❶ Glamorgan Street
❷ William Street
❸ Richardson Street
❹ A4067 Oystermouth Road (8 miles to M4 Junction 42)
❺ Swansea High Street BR Station (½ mile)
❻ Supervised Car Park
❼ North Bank

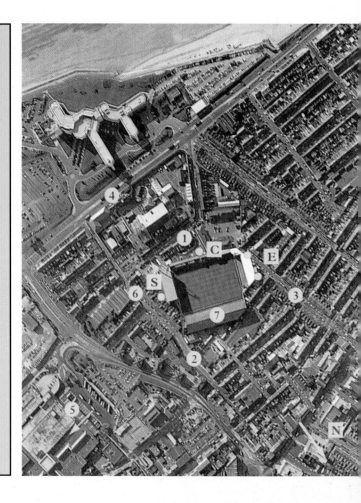

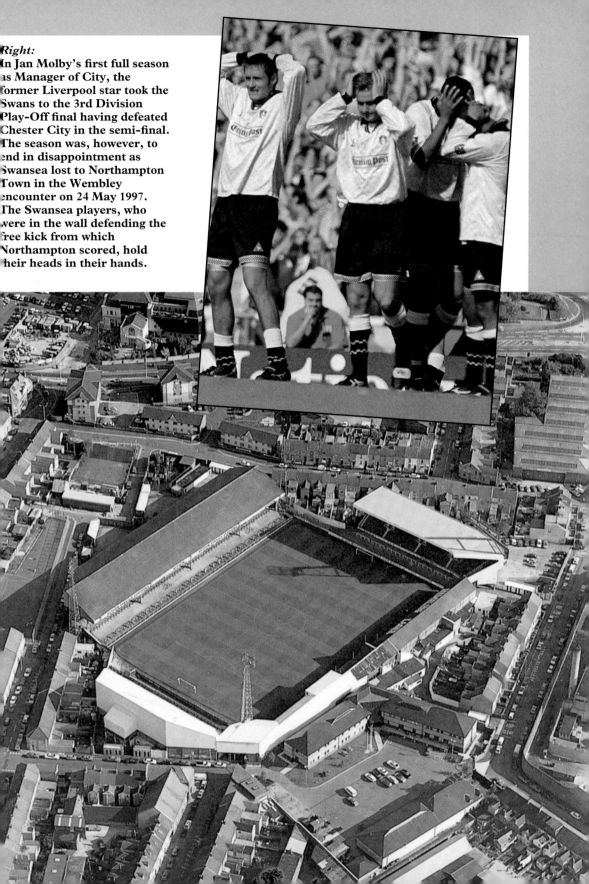

Right:
In Jan Molby's first full season as Manager of City, the former Liverpool star took the Swans to the 3rd Division Play-Off final having defeated Chester City in the semi-final. The season was, however, to end in disappointment as Swansea lost to Northampton Town in the Wembley encounter on 24 May 1997. The Swansea players, who were in the wall defending the free kick from which Northampton scored, hold their heads in their hands.

SWINDON TOWN

County Ground, County Road, Swindon, SN1 2ED

Tel No: 01793 430430
Advance Tickets Tel No: 01793 529000
Fax: 01793 536170
League: 1st Division
Brief History: Founded 1881. Former Grounds: Quarry Ground, Globe Field, Croft Ground, County Ground (adjacent current to Ground and now Cricket Ground), moved to current County Ground in 1896. Founder-members Third Division (1920). Record attendance 32,000
(Total) Current Capacity: 15,728 (all seated)
Visiting Supporters' Allocation: 2,180 (all seated)

Club Colours: Red shirts, red shorts
Nearest Railway Station: Swindon
Parking (Car): Town Centre
Parking (Coach/Bus): Adjacent car park
Police Force and Tel No: Wiltshire (01793 528111)
Disabled Visitors' Facilities
  Wheelchairs: Intel Stand
  Blind: Commentary available
Anticipated Development(s): The next stage of development at The County Ground will see the construction of a new roof over the Rover Family Stand (Town End). It is hoped to open the new facility during the 1997/98 season.

KEY

- **C** Club Offices
- **S** Club Shop
- **E** Entrance(s) for visiting supporters
- **R** Refreshment bars for visiting supporters
- **T** Toilets for visiting supporters

↑ North direction (approx)

- ❶ Shrivenham Road
- ❷ County Road
- ❸ A345 Queens Drive (M4 Junction 15 – 3½ miles)
- ❹ Swindon BR Station (½ mile)
- ❺ Town End
- ❻ Car Park
- ❼ County Cricket Ground
- ❽ Intel Stand
- ❾ Castrol Stand

Right:
Although Steve McMahon's Swindon Town ran away with the 2nd Division title at the end of 1995/96, the first season back in the 1st Division proved a struggle and, whilst never being sucked into the relegation battle, the team never achieved more than a mid-table position. David Kerslake is caught during the home game against eventual champions Bolton Wanderers on 22 December 1996.

TORQUAY UNITED

Plainmoor Ground, Torquay, TQ1 3PS

Tel No: 01803 328666
Advance Tickets Tel No: 01803 328666
Fax: 01803 323976
League: 3rd Division
Brief History: Founded 1898, as Torquay United, amalgamated with Ellacombe in 1910, changed name to Torquay Town. Amalgamated with Babbacombe in 1921, changed name to Torquay United. Former grounds: Teignmouth Road, Torquay Recreation Ground, Cricketfield Road & Torquay Cricket Ground, moved to Plainmoor (Ellacombe Ground) in 1910. Record attendance 21,908.
(Total) Current Capacity: 6,047 (2,359 seated)
Visiting Supporters' Allocation: 1,196 (200 seated)

Club Colours: Yellow with navy & white stripe shirts, navy shorts
Nearest Railway Station: Torquay (2 miles)
Parking (Car): Street parking
Parking (Coach/Bus): Lymington Road coach station
Police Force and Tel No: Devon & Cornwall (01803 214491)
Disabled Visitors' Facilities
  Wheelchairs: Ellacombe End
  Blind: Commentary available
Anticipated Development(s): The Babbacombe End, currently used by away supporters, is due to be replaced by a new 1,800 seat stand.

KEY

- **C** Club Offices
- **S** Club Shop
- **E** Entrance(s) for visiting supporters
- **R** Refreshment bars for visiting supporters
- **T** Toilets for visiting supporters

↑ North direction (approx)

❶ Warbro Road
❷ B3202 Marychurch Road
❸ Marnham Road
❹ Torquay BR Station (2 miles)
❺ To A38
❻ Babbacombe End

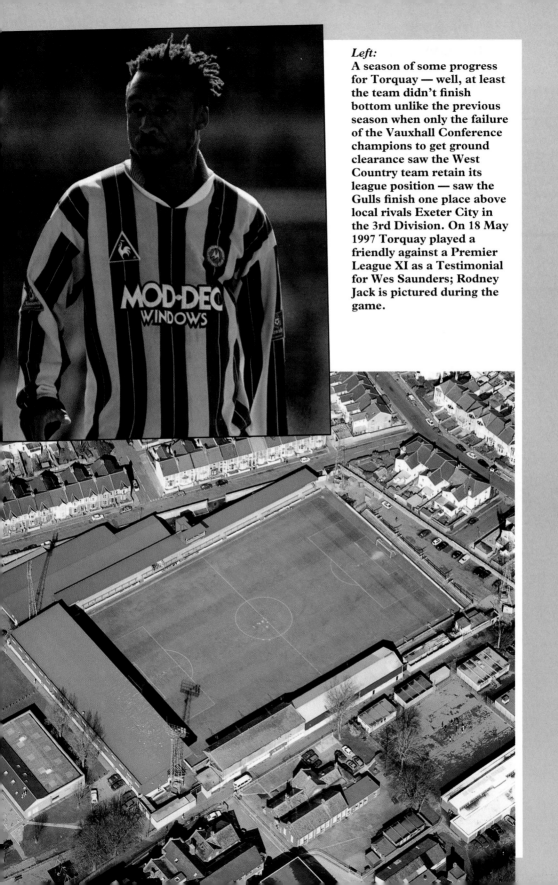

Left:
A season of some progress for Torquay — well, at least the team didn't finish bottom unlike the previous season when only the failure of the Vauxhall Conference champions to get ground clearance saw the West Country team retain its league position — saw the Gulls finish one place above local rivals Exeter City in the 3rd Division. On 18 May 1997 Torquay played a friendly against a Premier League XI as a Testimonial for Wes Saunders; Rodney Jack is pictured during the game.

TOTTENHAM HOTSPUR

White Hart Lane, 748 High Road, Tottenham, London N17 0AP

Tel No: 0181 365 5000
Advance Tickets Tel No: 0181 365 5050
Fax: 0181 365 5005
League: F. A. Premier
Brief History: Founded 1882 as 'Hotspur', changed name to Tottenham Hotspur in 1885. Former Grounds: Tottenham Marshes and Northumberland Park, moved to White Hart Lane in 1899. F. A. Cup winner 1901 (as a non-League club). Record attendance 75,038
(Total) Current Capacity: 33,083 (all seated)
Visiting Supporters' Allocation: 4,000
Club Colours: White shirts, navy blue shorts

Nearest Railway Station: White Hart Lane plus Seven Sisters & Manor House (tube)
Parking (Car): Street parking (min ¼ mile from ground)
Parking (Coach/Bus): Northumberland Park coach park
Police Force and Tel No: Metropolitan (0181 801 3443)
Disabled Visitors' Facilities
   Wheelchairs: North and South Stands (by prior arrangement)
   Blind: No special facility
Anticipated Development(s): None planned.

KEY

- **C** Club Offices
- **S** Club Shop
- **E** Entrance(s) for visiting supporters
- **R** Refreshment bars for visiting supporters
- **T** Toilets for visiting supporters

↑ North direction (approx)

- ❶ Park Lane
- ❷ A1010 High Road
- ❸ White Hart Lane BR Station
- ❹ Paxton Road
- ❺ Worcester Avenue
- ❻ West Stand
- ❼ South Stand

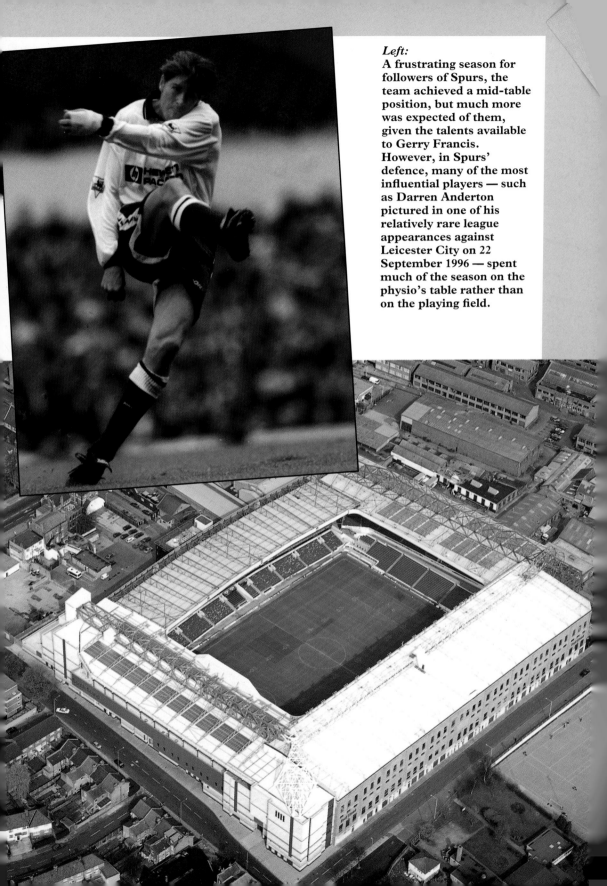

Left:
A frustrating season for followers of Spurs, the team achieved a mid-table position, but much more was expected of them, given the talents available to Gerry Francis. However, in Spurs' defence, many of the most influential players — such as Darren Anderton pictured in one of his relatively rare league appearances against Leicester City on 22 September 1996 — spent much of the season on the physio's table rather than on the playing field.

TRANMERE ROVERS

Prenton Park, Prenton Road West, Birkenhead, L42 9PN

Tel No: 0151 608 4194
Advance Tickets Tel No: 0151 609 0137
Fax: 0151 608 4385
League: 1st Division
Brief History: Founded 1884 as Belmont F.C., changed name to Tranmere Rovers in 1885 (not connected to earlier 'Tranmere Rovers'). Former grounds: Steele's Field and Ravenshaw's Field (also known as Old Prenton Park, ground of Tranmere Rugby Club), moved to (new) Prenton Park in 1911. Founder-members 3rd Division North (1921). Record attendance 24,424.

(Total) Current capacity: 16,912 (all seated)
Visiting Supporters' Allocation: Between 2,000 and 5,842 (all seated)
Club Colours: White shirts, white shorts
Nearest Railway Station: Hamilton Square or Rock Ferry
Parking (Car): Car park at Ground
Parking (Coach/Bus): Car park at Ground
Police Force and Tel No: Merseyside (0151 709 6010)
Disabled Visitors' Facilities
  Wheelchairs: Main Stand
  Blind: No special facility

KEY

C Club Offices
S Club Shop
E Entrance(s) for visiting supporters
R Refreshment bars for visiting supporters
T Toilets for visiting supporters

↑ North direction (approx)

❶ Car Park
❷ Prenton Road West
❸ Borough Road
❹ M53 Junction 4 (B5151) – 3 miles
❺ Birkenhead (1 mile)

Right:
With John Aldridge replacing long-serving John King as Rovers' Manager at the end of 1995/96, Tranmere were a team in transition. Tipped as potential relegation candidates, a position of mid-table security offers the potential for the team to make another effort in aiming for the Premiership. One piece of good news for Rovers' fans is that Aldridge — now aged 38 and pictured here in the home game against Sheffield United on 19 April 1997 — is planning to play for another season; his goal scoring instinct was certainly an influential part of Rovers' season in 1996/97.

WALSALL

Bescot Stadium, Bescot Crescent, Walsall, West Midlands, WS1 4S/

Tel No: 01922 22791
Advance Tickets Tel No: 01922 22791
Fax: 01922 613202
League: 2nd Division
Brief History: Founded 1888 as Walsall Town
Swifts (amalgamation of Walsall Town -
founded 1884 - and Walsall Swifts - founded
1885), changed name to Walsall in 1895.
Former Grounds: The Chuckery, West
Bromwich Road (twice), Hilary Street (later
named Fellows Park, twice), moved to Bescot
Stadium in 1990. Founder-members Second
Division (1892). Record attendance 10,628
(25,343 at Fellows Park).

(Total) Current Capacity: 9,000 (6,700 seated
Visiting Supporters' Allocation: 1,916 (1,916
seated)
Club Colours: Red shirts, Black shorts
Nearest Railway Station: Bescot
Parking (Car): Car park at Ground
Parking (Coach/Bus): Car park at Ground
Police Force and Tel No : West Midlands
(01922 38111)
Disabled Visitors' Facilities
Wheelchairs: Highgate Stand
Blind: No special facility

KEY

C Club Offices
S Club Shop
E Entrance(s) for visiting
supporters
R Refreshment bars for visiting
supporters
T Toilets for visiting supporters

↑ North direction (approx)

❶ Motorway M6
❷ M6 Junction 9
❸ Bescot BR Station
❹ Car Parks
❺ Bescot Crescent

Left:
At the end of the season Manager Chris Nicholl commented that either he went or the players did, following the Saddlers' failure to reach the 2nd Division Play-Offs. Given that the team only missed out on the Play-Offs by six points in its second season in the 2nd Division, Nicholl's attitude seems rather churlish. In slightly happier circumstances, Walsall's Charlie Ntamark is seen in action against 1st Division West Brom on 10 August 1996. Ultimately, it was the manager who went.

WATFORD

Vicarage Road Stadium, Watford, WD1 8ER

Tel No: 01923 496000
Advance Tickets Tel No: 01923 496010
Fax: 01923 496001
League: 2nd Division
Brief History: Founded 1898 as an amalgamation of West Herts (founded 1891) and Watford St. Mary's (founded early 1890s). Former Grounds: Wiggenhall Road (Watford St. Mary's) and West Herts Sports Ground, moved to Vicarage Road in 1922. Founder-members Third Division (1920). Record attendance 34,099.
(Total) Current Capacity: 22,000 (all seated)
Visiting Supporters' Allocation: 10,276 in the Lower Road and Rookery End

Club Colours: Yellow shirts, red shorts
Nearest Railway Station: Watford High Street or Watford Junction.
Parking (Car): Nearby multi-storey car park in town centre (10 mins walk)
Parking (Coach/Bus): Cardiff Road car park
Police Force and Tel No: Hertfordshire (01923 244444)
Disabled Visitors' Facilities
  Wheelchairs: Corner East Stand and South Stand (special enclosure for approx. 24 wheelchairs), plus enclosure in North East Corner
  Blind: Commentary available in the East Stand (20 seats, free of charge)

KEY
- **C** Club Offices
- **S** Club Shop
- **E** Entrance(s) for visiting supporters
- **R** Refreshment bars for visiting supporters
- **T** Toilets for visiting supporters

↑ North direction (approx)

❶ Vicarage Road
❷ Occupation Road
❸ Rous Stand
❹ Town Centre (1/2 mile) – Car Parks, High Street BR Station

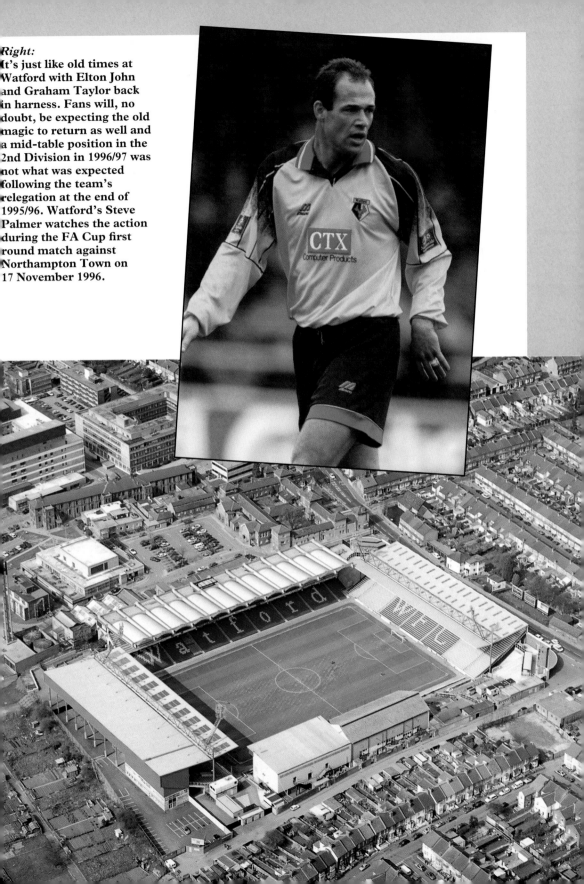

Right:
It's just like old times at Watford with Elton John and Graham Taylor back in harness. Fans will, no doubt, be expecting the old magic to return as well and a mid-table position in the 2nd Division in 1996/97 was not what was expected following the team's relegation at the end of 1995/96. Watford's Steve Palmer watches the action during the FA Cup first round match against Northampton Town on 17 November 1996.

WEST BROMWICH ALBION

The Hawthorns, Halfords Lane, West Bromwich, West Midlands, B71 4LF

Tel No: 0121 525 8888
Advance Tickets Tel No: 0121 553 5472
Fax: 0121 553 6634
Ticket Office Fax: 0121 553 4204
E-Mail: baggies@wba.co.uk
League: 1st Division
Brief History: Founded 1879. Former Grounds: Coopers Hill, Dartmouth Park, Four Acres, Stoney Lane, moved to the Hawthorns in 1900. Founder-members of Football League (1888). Record attendance 64,815.
(Total) Current Capacity: 25,000 (all seated)
Visiting Supporters' Allocation: 2,100

Club Colours: Navy blue & white striped shirts, white shorts
Nearest Railway Station: Hawthorns
Parking (Car): Halfords Lane & Rainbow Stand car parks.
Parking (Coach/Bus): Rainbow Stand car park
Police Force and Tel No: West Midlands (0121 554 3414)
Disabled Visitors' Facilities
  Wheelchairs: Apollo 2000 and Travel West Midlands Community Stands
  Blind: Facility available

KEY
C Club Offices
S Club Shop
E Entrance(s) for visiting supporters
T Toilets for visiting supporters

⬆ North direction (approx)

❶ A41 Birmingham Road
❷ M5 Junction 1
❸ Birmingham centre (4 miles)
❹ Halfords Lane
❺ Main Stand
❻ Smethwick End
❼ Rolfe Street, Smethwick BR Station (1½ miles)
❽ The Hawthorns BR Station

Left:
Another season of under-achievement saw the Baggies dispense with one Manager and face the possibility that his successor, ex-Blackburn boss Ray Harford, would follow suit unless money was made available to strengthen the squad. One of the increasing foreign legion in the Nationwide League was Dutchman Richard Sneekes, seen here in league action against Port Vale on 9 September 1996.

WEST HAM UNITED

Boleyn Ground, Green Street, Upton Park, London, E13 9AZ

Tel No: 0181 548 2748
Advance Tickets Tel No: 0181 548 2700
Fax: 0181 548 2758
League: F. A. Premier
Brief History: Founded 1895 as Thames Ironworks, changed name to West Ham United in 1900. Former Grounds: Hermit Road, Browning Road, The Memorial Ground, moved to Boleyn Ground in 1904. Record attendance 42,322.
(Total) Current Capacity: 26,014 (all seated)
Visiting Supporters' Allocation: 3,700
Club Colours: Claret & blue shirts, white shorts.
Nearest Railway Station: Barking BR, Upton Park (tube)

Parking (Car): Street parking
Parking (Coach/Bus): As directed by police
Police Force and Tel No: Metropolitan (0181 593 8232)
Disabled Visitors' Facilities
  Wheelchairs: West Lower, Bobby Moore and Centenary Stands
  Blind: Commentaries available
Anticipated Development(s): There are tentative plans for the in-filling of the corners or of redevelopment of the West Stand but when this work will be undertaken has yet to be confirmed.

KEY

C Club Offices
S Club Shop
E Entrance(s) for visiting supporters

↑ North direction (approx)

❶ A124 Barking Road
❷ Green Street
❸ North Stand
❹ Upton Park Tube Station (¼ mile)
❺ Barking BR Station (1 mile)
❻ Bobby Moore Stand
❼ East Stand
❽ West Stand

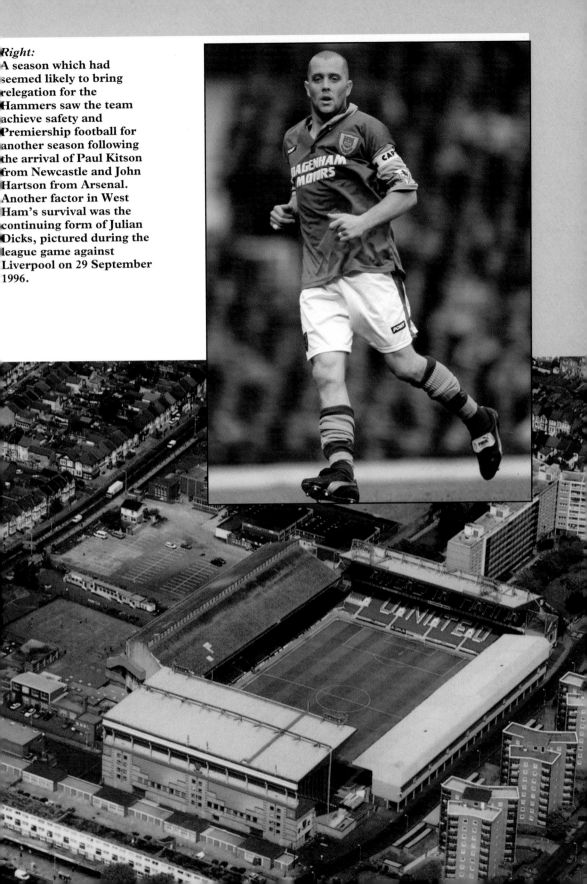

Right:
A season which had seemed likely to bring relegation for the Hammers saw the team achieve safety and Premiership football for another season following the arrival of Paul Kitson from Newcastle and John Hartson from Arsenal. Another factor in West Ham's survival was the continuing form of Julian Dicks, pictured during the league game against Liverpool on 29 September 1996.

WIGAN ATHLETIC

Springfield Park, Wigan, Lancs, WN6 7BA

Tel No: 01942 244433
Advance Tickets Tel No: 01942 244433
Fax: 01942 494654
League: 2nd Division
Brief History: Founded 1932. Springfield Park used by former club Wigan Borough (Football League 1921-31) but unrelated to current club. Elected to Football League in 1978 (the last club to be elected rather than promoted). Record attendance 27,500.
(Total) Current Capacity: 7,466 (1,128 seated)
Visiting Supporters' Allocation: 1,730 (263 seated)
Club Colours: Blue, green and white stripes shirt, white and green shorts
Nearest Railway Station: Wallgate and North Western (1 mile)

Parking (Car): Street parking
Parking (Coach/Bus): At Ground
Police Force and Tel No: Greater Manchester (01942 244981)
Disabled Visitors' Facilities
  Wheelchairs: Phoenix Stand side
  Blind: Commentary available, book in advance and bring own headphones.
Anticipated Development(s): Following the collapse of plans to ground-share with Wigan RLFC, Athletic are now planning a new 25,000-seat stadium that will be shared with Orell RUFC. It is possible that the new ground will be opened either for, or during, the 1998/99 season.

KEY

C Club Offices
E Entrance(s) for visiting supporters
R Refreshment bars for visiting supporters
T Toilets for visiting supporters

↑ North direction (approx)

❶ Private Car Park
❷ Springfield Road
❸ St. Andrews Drive
❹ Wallgate and North Western BR Stations (1 mile)

Left:
Completing a clean sweep for the northwest of England in the divisional championships, Wigan Athletic took the 3rd Division title on goal difference from Fulham. Despite the (shirt-pulling) attentions of the Mansfield player, Athletic's David Lowe makes a determined run during the 3rd Division encounter on 3 May 1997.

WIMBLEDON

Selhurst Park, London, SE25 6PY

Tel No: 0181 771 2233
Advance Tickets Tel No: 0181 771 8841
Fax: 0181 768 0641
League: F.A. Premier
Brief History: Founded 1889 as Wimbledon Old Centrals, changed name to Wimbledon in 1905. Former Grounds: Wimbledon Common, Pepy's Road, Grand Drive, Merton Hall Road, Malden Wanderers Cricket Ground & Plough Lane. Moved to Selhurst Park (Crystal Palace F.C. Ground) in 1991. Elected to Football League in 1977. Record attendance (Plough Lane) 18,000.
(Total) Current Capacity: 26,296 (all seated)
Visiting Supporters' Allocation: Approx 3,000
Club Colours: Blue shirts, blue shorts

Nearest Railway Station: Selhurst, Norwood Junction & Thornton Heath
Parking (Car): Street parking & Sainsbury's car park
Parking (Coach/Bus): Thornton Heath
Police Force and Tel No: Metropolitan (0181 649 1391)
Disabled Visitors' Facilities
  Wheelchairs: Park Road
  Blind: Commentary available
Anticipated Development(s): Nothing confirmed following the completion of the Holmesdale Stand. As to whether Wimbledon will continue to play at Selhurst Park, nothing has yet been decided.

KEY

C Club Offices
S Club Shop
E Entrance(s) for visiting supporters
T Toilets for visiting supporters

⬆ North direction (approx)

❶ Whitehorse Lane
❷ Park Road
❸ A213 Selhurst Road
❹ Selhurst BR Station (1/2 mile)
❺ Norwood Junction BR Station (1/4 mile)
❻ Thornton Heath BR Station (1/2 mile)
❼ Car Park (Sainsbury's)
❽ Holmesdale Stand

Right:
A season which started disastrously, which then brought the Dons to two cup semi-finals and the fringes of achieving a UEFA cup place, culminated in Roy Kinnear's team gaining nothing except the plaudits of many commentators, for whom the Manager's skill in obtaining considerable success with limited resources deserved great praise. Efan Ekoku, caught during the Premiership game with Newcastle United on 23 March 1997, was one of the Dons' success stories during an ultimately frustrating season.

WOLVERHAMPTON WANDERERS

Molineux Ground, Waterloo Road, Wolverhampton, WV1 4QR

Tel No: 01902 655000
Advance Tickets Tel No: 01902 653653
Fax: 01902 687006
E-Mail: wolvesinfo@mbcis.co.uk
League: 1st Division
Brief History: Founded 1877 as St. Lukes, combined with Goldthorn Hill to become Wolverhampton Wanderers in 1884. Former Grounds: Old Windmill Field, John Harper's Field and Dudley Road, moved to Molineux in 1889. Founder-members Football League (1888). Record attendance 61,315
(Total) Current Capacity: 28,500 (all seated)

Visiting Supporters' Allocation: 1,500 in John Harris stand or 3,000 in lower tier of John Ireland stand
Club Colours: Gold shirts, black shorts
Nearest Railway Station: Wolverhampton
Parking (Car): West Park and adjacent North Bank
Parking (Coach/Bus): As directed by Police
Police Force and Tel No: West Midlands (01902 27851)
Disabled Visitors' Facilities
  Wheelchairs: 115 places on three sides
  Blind: Commentary (by prior arrangement)

KEY

C Club Offices
S Club Shop
E Entrance(s) for visiting supporters
R Refreshment bars for visiting supporters
T Toilets for visiting supporters

↑ North direction (approx)

❶ Stan Cullis Stand
❷ John Ireland Stand
❸ Billy Wright Stand
❹ Ring Road – St. Peters
❺ Waterloo Road
❻ A449 Stafford Street
❼ BR Station (¹/₂ mile)
❽ John Harris Stand
❾ Molineux Street
❿ Molineux Way

Left:
A change of Manager, with Mark McGhee having replaced Graham Taylor towards the end of the 1995/96 season, but still high-spending Wolves failed to achieve one of the two automatic promotion places from the 1st Division. Finishing third, the team faced Crystal Palace in the divisional Play-Off semi-finals and lost. It will be interesting to see, if Wolves continue to underachieve, how long the club will be able to hang on to ambitious players like Dean Richards, pictured here in the game against Reading on 5 October 1996.

WREXHAM

Racecourse Ground, Mold Road, Wrexham, Clwyd LL11 2AN

Tel No: 01978 262129
Advance Tickets Tel No: 01978 262129
Fax: 01978 357821
League: 2nd Division
Brief History: Founded 1873 (oldest Football
Club in Wales). Former Ground: Acton Park,
permanent move to Racecourse Ground
c.1900. Founder-members Third Division
North (1921). Record attendance 34,445.
(Total) Current Capacity: 12,024 (5,024
seated)
Visiting Supporters' Allocation: 2,840 (2,200
seated)

Club Colours: Red shirts, white shorts
Nearest Railway Station: Wrexham General
Parking (Car): (Nearby) Town car parks
Parking (Coach/Bus): As directed by Police
Police Force and Tel No: Wrexham Division
(01978 290222)
Disabled Visitors' Facilities
Wheelchairs: Mold Road Side
Blind: No special facility
Anticipated development(s): Work is still
about to start on a new 4,000 seat stand.

KEY

C Club Offices
S Club Shop
E Entrance(s) for visiting
supporters
R Refreshment bars for visiting
supporters
T Toilets for visiting supporters

⬆ North direction (approx)

❶ Wrexham General BR Station
❷ A541 – Mold Road
❸ Wrexham Town Centre
❹ Car Park
❺ Kop Town End

Right:
Whilst the highest placed Welsh team in the Nationwide League achieved fame through its cup exploits, eventually losing 1-0 to fellow cup heroes Chesterfield in the Sixth Round, Brian Flynn would have traded some of that success to sustaining a challenge for one of the 2nd Division Play-Off spots. As it was, Wrexham finished eighth in the division and will hope that 1997/98 will bring greater success. Wrexham's goal scorer in the victorious cup tie against West Ham on 4 January 1997 battles in the snow with Hammers' Ian Bishop.

WYCOMBE WANDERERS

Adams Park, Hillbottom Road, Sands, High Wycombe, Bucks, HP12 4HJ.

Tel No: 01494 472100
Advance Tickets Tel No: 01494 441118
Fax: 01494 527633
League: 2nd Division
Brief History: Founded 1884. Former Grounds: The Rye, Spring Meadows, Loakes Park, moved to Adams Park 1990. Promoted to Football League 1993. Record attendance 15,678 (Loakes Park)
(Total) Current Capacity: 10,000 (7,306 seated)
Visiting Supporters' Allocation: 1,049
Club Colours: Sky blue with navy blue quartered shirts, Blue shorts.

Nearest Railway Station: High Wycombe (2¹/2 miles)
Parking (Car): At Ground and Street parking
Parking (Coach/Bus): At Ground
Police Force and Tel No: Thames Valley 01296 396534
Disabled Visitors' Facilities
  Wheelchairs: Special shelter - Main Stand, Hillbottom Road end
  Blind: Commentary available
Anticipated Development(s): Nothing further planned after completion of South (Servispak) Stand.

KEY
C Club Offices
S Club Shop
E Entrance(s) for visiting supporters
R Refreshment bars for visiting supporters
T Toilets for visiting supporters

↑ North direction (approx)

❶ Car Park
❷ Hillbottom Road (Industrial Estate)
❸ M40 Junction 4 (approx. 2 miles)
❹ Wycombe Town Centre (approx. 2¹/2 miles)
❺ Servispak Stand
❻ Roger Vere Stand (away)

Left:

Another season of toil for Wanderers saw the team in the 2nd Division relegation spots for much of the year. The club, aided by a victory over fellow strugglers Shrewsbury Town, was able to retain its 2nd Division spot for another year; fans will, however, be expecting the team to emulate the success brought under Martin O'Neills's managership in 1997/98. John Williams seems in determined mood in this contest.

YORK CITY

Bootham Crescent, York, YO3 7AQ

Tel No: 01904 624447
Advance Tickets Tel No: 01904 624447
Fax: 01904 631457
League: 2nd Division
Brief History: Founded 1922. Former ground: Fulfordgate Ground, moved to Bootham Crescent in 1932. Record attendance 28,123.
(Total) Current Capacity: 9,459 (3,670 seated)
Visiting Supporters' Allocation: 3,500 (630 seated)

Club Colours: Red with blue and white trim shirts and shorts
Nearest Railway Station: York
Parking (Car): Street parking
Parking (Coach/Bus): As directed by Police
Police Force and Tel No: North Yorkshire (01904 631321)
Disabled Visitors' Facilities
   Wheelchairs: In front of Family Stand
   Blind: Commentary available

KEY

C Club Offices
S Club Shop
E Entrance(s) for visiting supporters
R Refreshment bars for visiting supporters
T Toilets for visiting supporters

⬆ North direction (approx)

❶ Bootham Crescent
❷ Grosvenor Road
❸ Burton Stone Lane
❹ York BR Station (1 mile)

Right:
A disappointing season for York saw the team only evade relegation by one place. Graeme Murty keeps a wary eye on the ball in this Coca-Cola Cup Third Round match against Leicester City — the eventual winners of the competition — on 22 October 1996.

OXFORD UNITED

Manor Ground, London Road, Headington, Oxford, OX3 7RS

Tel No: 01865 61503
Advance Tickets Tel No: 01865 61503
League: 1st Division
Brief History: Founded 1893 as Headington (later Headington United), changed name to Oxford United in 1960. Former grounds: Brittania Inn Field, Headington Quarry, Wooten's Field, Manor Ground, The Paddocks, moved back to Manor Ground in 1925. Record attendance 22,730.
(Total) Current Capacity: 9,572 (6,769 seated)
Visiting Supporters' Allocation: 2,649
Club Colours: Yellow with navy trim shirts, navy with yellow trim shorts.

Nearest Railway Station: Oxford (3 miles)
Parking (Car): Street parking
Parking (Coach/Bus): Headley Way
Police Force and Tel No: Thames Valley (01865 777501)
Disabled Visitors' Facilities
  Wheelchairs: Main Stand
  Blind: No special facility
Anticipated Development(s): See Page 122 for details of the new ground.

KEY

C Club Offices
E Entrance(s) for visiting supporters
R Refreshment bars for visiting supporters

North direction (approx)

❶ A420 London Road
❷ Osler Road
❸ To City Centre and Oxford BR Station (3 miles)
❹ To A40 and Ring Road (¾ mile)
❺ Cuckoo Lane